RENEWED
EACH
DAY

Other Books in the New Perspectives™ Series

Free from the Past
Bible Promises for Adult Children of Alcoholics
Healing for Today, Hope for Tomorrow
Bible Promises for Overcoming Codependency
Hope for the Hungry Heart
Bible Promises for Overeaters

New Perspectives™

RENEWED
EACH
DAY

Bible Promises for Overcoming
Chemical Dependencies

Compiled by
Gary Wilde

A
JANET
THOMA
BOOK

Thomas Nelson Publishers
Nashville

Published in Nashville, Tennessee, by Thomas
Nelson, Inc., and distributed in Canada by Lawson
Falle, Ltd., Cambridge, Ontario.

Scripture quotations are from the NEW KING JAMES
VERSION of the Bible. Copyright © 1979, 1980, 1982,
Thomas Nelson, Inc., Publishers.

Library of Congress Cataloging-in-Publication Data

Wilde, Gary.
  Renewed each day : Bible promises for
overcoming chemical dependencies / compiled by
Gary Wilde.
      p.   cm. — (New perspectives)
  ISBN 0-8407-3246-5
  1. Promises—Biblical teaching.   2. Substance
abuse—Patients—Prayer-books and devotions.
I. Title. II. Series.
BS680.P68W55   1991
242'.4—dc20   92-117
                                                    CIP

Printed in the United States of America
1 2 3 4 5 6 7 — 96 95 94 93 92

CONTENTS

Introduction

You have chosen to walk the road to recovery from chemical addiction—the path to serenity. At times along the way you will face seemingly impossible challenges and some painful realities in order to receive the health and peace you are longing for. *Renewed Each Day* gives you the encouragement and strength you need for your journey with Scripture promises from the New King James Version of the Bible.

Each chapter takes you through a different step of recovery—seeing your true self, surveying your relationship history, breaking the addiction cycle, saying good-bye, experiencing grief, developing new self-perceptions. And the Scripture passages within each chapter are fertile ground for you to begin sowing new choices and reaping lifelong benefits. You will find freedom from shame and guilt in verses of God's unconditional love and hope in God's promise to be a perfect parent. You will see the necessity of accountability and gain the wisdom you need to maintain your new lifestyle.

You may want to read this book from beginning to end. Or you may choose to turn to the section that relates to where you are today and read and meditate on those passages. But however you choose to use this book, keep it nearby for you to turn to anytime of the day.

Discover new perspectives for your life as you read God's words in *Renewed Each Day*.

CHAPTER

1

Exploration and Discovery

The road to recovery leads us on a journey into the self. Those who choose to begin this journey may at first be surprised at the amount of inner reflection and self-examination required. Yet, we either continue on the route of escape (through the addiction of our choice, because of its anesthetizing qualities), or we choose to "wake up" and face ourselves.

Because many of us are so used to running from emotional hurt, we need to spend a good amount of time simply exploring our inner selves for the places where it hides. Pain that is covered over needs more and more tranquilizing to keep it in check. Invite it to bubble to the surface!

Certainly, no one would claim that finding and facing such pain is easy or pleasant. It may be the hardest thing a person can ever do. But those who have entered recovery do claim that feeling the pain is ultimately preferable to denying it. By feeling it and going through it, we walk a path that leads to a new sensation, one we may have long forgotten—deep joy.

Opening Up to My True Self

"No one, when he has lit a lamp, puts it in a secret place or under a basket, but on a lampstand, that those who come in may see the light. The lamp of the body is the eye. Therefore, when your eye is good, your whole body also is full of light. But when your eye is bad, your body also is full of darkness. Therefore take heed that the light which is in you is not darkness. If then your whole body is full of light, having no part dark, the whole body will be full of light, as when the bright shining of a lamp gives you light."

—LUKE 11:33–36

"For there is nothing covered that will not be revealed, nor hidden that will not be known. Therefore whatever you have spoken in the dark will be heard in the light, and what you have spoken in the ear in inner rooms will be proclaimed on the housetops."

—LUKE 12:2–3

■ *Finding and Facing Inner Pain*

O my soul, my soul!
I am pained in my very heart!
My heart makes a noise in me;
I cannot hold my peace.

—JEREMIAH 4:19

Why is my pain perpetual
And my wound incurable,
Which refuses to be healed?
Will You surely be to me like an unreliable
    stream,
As waters that fail?

—JEREMIAH 15:18

When I thought how to understand this,
It was too painful for me

—PSALM 73:16

For my iniquities have gone over my head;
Like a heavy burden they are too heavy for
    me.
My wounds are foul and festering
Because of my foolishness.
I am troubled, I am bowed down greatly;
I go mourning all the day long.
For my loins are full of inflammation,
And there is no soundness in my flesh.

I am feeble and severely broken;
I groan because of the turmoil of my heart.

—PSALM 38:4–8

■ *Examining Myself for the Causes of My Problems*

. . . Pharisees look only at externals . . .

"Woe to you, scribes and Pharisees, hypocrites! For you pay tithe of mint and anise and cumin, and have neglected the weightier matters of the law: justice and mercy and faith. These you ought to have done, without leaving the others undone. Blind guides, who strain out a gnat and swallow a camel! Woe to you, scribes and Pharisees, hypocrites! For you cleanse the outside of the cup and dish, but inside they are full of extortion and self-indulgence. Blind Pharisee, first cleanse the inside of the cup and dish, that the outside of them may be clean also. Woe to you, scribes and Pharisees, hypocrites! For you are like whitewashed tombs which indeed appear beautiful outwardly, but inside are full of dead men's bones and all uncleanness. Even so you also outwardly appear righteous to men, but inside you are full of hypocrisy and lawlessness."

—MATTHEW 23:23–28

. . . But we must look objectively within.

For we dare not class ourselves or compare ourselves with those who commend themselves. But they, measuring themselves by themselves, and comparing themselves among themselves, are not wise.

—2 CORINTHIANS 10:12

Examine yourselves as to whether you are in the faith. Prove yourselves. Do you not know yourselves, that Jesus Christ is in you?—unless indeed you are disqualified.

—2 CORINTHIANS 13:5

Now the works of the flesh are evident, which are: adultery, fornication, uncleanness, lewdness, idolatry, sorcery, hatred, contentions, jealousies, outbursts of wrath, selfish ambitions, dissensions, heresies, envy, murders, drunkenness, revelries, and the like; of which I tell you beforehand, just as I also told you in time past, that those who practice such things will not inherit the kingdom of God.

—GALATIANS 5:19–21

For if anyone thinks himself to be something, when he is nothing, he deceives himself. But let each one examine his own work, and then he will have rejoicing in himself alone, and not in another. For each one shall bear his own load.

—GALATIANS 6:3–5

■ Dealing with Secret Faults

Who can understand his errors?
Cleanse me from secret faults.

Keep back Your servant also from
   presumptuous sins;
Let them not have dominion over me. Then I
   shall be blameless,
And I shall be innocent of great transgression.
Let the words of my mouth and the
   meditation of my heart
Be acceptable in Your sight, O LORD, my
   strength and my redeemer.

—PSALM 19:12–14

Ananias and Sapphira Covered Up . . .

But a certain man named Ananias, with Sapphira his wife, sold a possession. And he kept back part of the proceeds, his wife also being aware of it, and brought a certain part and laid it at the apostles' feet. But Peter said, "Ananias, why has Satan filled your heart to lie to the Holy Spirit and keep back part of the price of the land for yourself? While it remained, was it not your own? And after it was sold, was it not in your own control? Why have you conceived this thing in your heart? You have not lied to men but to God." Then Ananias, hearing these words, fell down and breathed his last. So great fear came upon all those who heard these things. And the young men arose and wrapped him up, carried him out, and buried him. Now it was about three hours later when his wife came in, not knowing what had happened. And Peter answered her, "Tell me whether you sold the land for so much?" She said, "Yes, for so much." Then Peter said to her, "How is it that you have agreed together to test the Spirit of the Lord? Look, the feet of those who have buried your husband are at the door, and they will carry you out." Then immediately she fell down at his feet and breathed her last. And the young men came in and found her dead, and carrying her out, buried her by her husband. So great fear came upon all the church and upon all who heard these things.

—ACTS 5:1–11

. . . But We Must Discern the Spirit of Truth and Error

Beloved, do not believe every spirit, but test the spirits, whether they are of God; because many false prophets have gone out into the world. By this you know the Spirit of God: Every spirit that confesses that Jesus Christ has come in the flesh is of God, and every spirit that does not confess that Jesus Christ has come in the flesh is not of God. And this is the spirit of the Antichrist, which you have heard was coming, and is now already in the world. You are of God, little children, and have overcome them, because He who is in you is greater than he who is in the world. They are of the world. Therefore they speak as of the world, and the world hears them. We are of God. He who knows God hears us; he who is not of God does not hear us. By this we know the spirit of truth and the spirit of error.

—1 JOHN 4:1-6

■ Confronting Inner Sin

"If your right eye causes you to sin, pluck it out and cast it from you; for it is more profitable for you that one of your members perish, than for your whole body to be cast into hell. And if your right hand causes you to sin, cut it off and cast it from you; for it is more profitable for you that one of your members perish, than for your whole body to be cast into hell."

—MATTHEW 5:29-30

For I know that in me (that is, in my flesh) nothing good dwells; for to will is present with me, but how to perform what is good I do not find. For the good that I will to do, I do not do; but the evil I will not to do, that I practice. Now if I do what I will not to do, it is no longer I who do it, but sin that dwells in me.

—ROMANS 7:18-20

But fornication and all uncleanness or covetousness, let it not even be named among you, as is fitting for saints; neither filthiness, nor foolish talking, nor coarse jesting, which are not fitting, but rather giving of thanks. For this you know, that no fornicator, unclean person, nor covetous man, who is an idolater, has any inheritance in the kingdom of Christ and God. Let no one deceive you with empty words, for because of these things the wrath of God comes upon the sons of disobedience. Therefore do not be partakers with them. . . . And do not be drunk with wine, in which is dissipation; but be filled with the Spirit.

—EPHESIANS 5:3–7, 18

■ Being Open to Correction

He who keeps instruction is in the way of life,
But he who refuses reproof goes astray.

—PROVERBS 10:17

He who despises the word will be destroyed,
But he who fears the commandment will be
rewarded.

—PROVERBS 13:13

The backslider in heart will be filled with his
own ways,
But a good man will be satisfied from above.

—PROVERBS 14:14

The ear that hears the rebukes of life
Will abide among the wise.
He who disdains instruction despises his own
soul,
But he who heeds reproof gets understanding.

The fear of the LORD is the instruction of
 wisdom,
And before honor is humility.

—PROVERBS 15:31–33

He who is often reproved, and hardens his
 neck,
Will suddenly be destroyed, and that without
 remedy. . . .
A man's pride will bring him low,
But the humble in spirit will retain honor.

—PROVERBS 29:1, 23

Opening Up to My True Source

In the beginning God created. . . .
Then God said, "Let Us make man in Our
image, according to Our likeness; let them have
dominion over the fish of the sea, over the birds of
the air, and over the cattle, over all the earth and
over every creeping thing that creeps on the
earth." So God created man in His own image; in
the image of God He created him; male and female He created them.

—GENESIS 1:1, 26–27

When I consider Your heavens, the work of
 Your fingers,
The moon and the stars, which You have
 ordained,
What is man that You are mindful of him,

And the son of man that You visit him?
For You have made him a little lower than the
   angels,
And You have crowned him with glory and
   honor.
You have made him to have dominion over the
   works of Your hands;
You have put all things under his feet,
All sheep and oxen—
Even the beasts of the field,
The birds of the air,
And the fish of the sea
That pass through the paths of the seas.
O LORD, our Lord,
How excellent is Your name in all the earth!
                                   —PSALM 8:3–9

■ *God Sees!*

"Can anyone hide himself in secret places,
So I shall not see him?" says the LORD;
"Do I not fill heaven and earth?" says the
   LORD.

                                   —JEREMIAH 23:24

Woe to those who seek deep to hide their
   counsel far from the LORD,
And their works are in the dark;
They say, "Who sees us?" and, "Who knows
   us?"
Surely you have things turned around!
Shall the potter be esteemed as the clay;

For shall the thing made say of him who made
    it,
"He did not make me"?
Or shall the thing formed say of him who
    formed it,
"He has no understanding"?

—ISAIAH 29:15–16

■ God Knows My Inner Life

O LORD, You have searched me and known
    me.
You know my sitting down and my rising up;
You understand my thought afar off.
You comprehend my path and my lying
    down,
And are acquainted with all my ways.
For there is not a word on my tongue,
But behold, O LORD, You know it altogether.
You have hedged me behind and before,
And laid Your hand upon me.
Such knowledge is too wonderful for me;
It is high, I cannot attain it.
Where can I go from Your Spirit?
Or where can I flee from Your presence?
If I ascend into heaven, You are there;
If I make my bed in hell, behold, You are
    there.
If I take the wings of the morning,
And dwell in the uttermost parts of the sea,
Even there Your hand shall lead me,
And Your right hand shall hold me.

If I say, "Surely the darkness shall fall on me,"
Even the night shall be light about me;
Indeed, the darkness shall not hide from You,
But the night shines as the day;
The darkness and the light are both alike to
    You.
For You have formed my inward parts;
You have covered me in my mother's womb.
I will praise You, for I am fearfully and
    wonderfully made;
Marvelous are Your works, And that my soul
    knows very well.
My frame was not hidden from You,
When I was made in secret,
And skillfully wrought in the lowest parts of
    the earth.
Your eyes saw my substance, being yet
    unformed.
And in Your book they all were written,
The days fashioned for me,
When as yet there were none of them. . . .
Search me, O God, and know my heart;
Try me, and know my anxieties;
And see if there is any wicked way in me,
And lead me in the way everlasting.
                            —PSALM 139:1–16, 23–24

■ *God Helps Me See My True Self*

"Will it be well when [God] searches you out?
Or can you mock Him as one mocks a man?
He will surely reprove you

If you secretly show partiality.
Will not His excellence make you afraid,
And the dread of Him fall upon you? . . .

"He also shall be my salvation,
For a hypocrite could not come before
  Him. . . .

"Only two things do not do to me,
Then I will not hide myself from You:
Withdraw Your hand far from me,
And let not the dread of You make me afraid.
Then call, and I will answer;
Or let me speak, then You respond to me.
How many are my iniquities and sins?
Make me know my transgression and my sin."
—JOB 13:9–11, 16, 20–23

Surveying My Relationship History

Our relationships, particularly our early family relationships, have made us what we are today. In a sense, we actually carry those relationships around with us: My boss at work points out a simple mistake; yet I feel deep shame. Is it really a disapproving parent that I still hear scolding me? I lash out at my children, verbally and physically. Can I recall the scenes from my childhood when the same things happened to me?

If it's true that early relationships have such ongoing impact today, surely it's best to explore the dynamics of those early interactions. We can find out what role we played in our family; we can discover how we still conform ourselves to that role so automatically when daily pressure builds.

People who thoroughly survey their relationship histories begin "catching" themselves, recognizing when they're falling into old patterns of reaction and behavior that really have little to do with the present circumstances.

Considering Your Role in Your Dysfunctional Family

■ *Were you the RESCUER?*

Joseph situated his father and his brothers, and gave them a possession in the land of Egypt, in the best of the land, in the land of Rameses, as Pharaoh had commanded. Then Joseph provided his father, his brothers, and all his father's household with bread, according to the number in their families. . . . And Joseph gathered up all the money that was found in the land of Egypt and in the land of Canaan, for the grain which they bought; and Joseph brought the money into Pharaoh's house. . . . Then Joseph said to the people, "Indeed I have bought you and your land this day for Pharaoh. Look, here is seed for you, and you shall sow the land. . . ." So they said, "You have saved our lives. . . ."

—GENESIS 47:11–12, 14, 23, 25a

■ *. . . Let God Be the Rescuer!*

Therefore say to the children of Israel: "I am the LORD; I will bring you out from under the burdens of the Egyptians, I will rescue you from their

bondage, and I will redeem you with an outstretched arm and with great judgments."

—EXODUS 6:6

Oh, give thanks to the Lord of lords!
For His mercy endures forever:
To Him who alone does great wonders,
For His mercy endures forever;
To Him who by wisdom made the heavens,
For His mercy endures forever;
To Him who laid out the earth above the
     waters,
For His mercy endures forever;
To Him who made great lights,
For His mercy endures forever—
The sun to rule by day,
For His mercy endures forever;
The moon and stars to rule by night,
For His mercy endures forever.
To Him who struck Egypt in their firstborn,
For His mercy endures forever;
And brought out Israel from among them,
For His mercy endures forever;
With a strong hand, and with an outstretched
     arm,
For His mercy endures forever;
To Him who divided the Red Sea in two,
For His mercy endures forever;
And made Israel pass through the midst of it,
For His mercy endures forever;
But overthrew Pharaoh and his army in the
     Red Sea,

For His mercy endures forever;
To Him who led His people through the
    wilderness,
For His mercy endures forever. . . .
[To Him] Who remembered us in our lowly
    state,
For His mercy endures forever;
And rescued us from our enemies,
For His mercy endures forever.

—PSALM 136:3–16, 23–24

■ Were You the SCAPEGOAT?

He shall take the two goats and present them before the LORD at the door of the tabernacle of meeting. Then Aaron shall cast lots for the two goats: one lot for the LORD and the other lot for the scapegoat. And Aaron shall bring the goat on which the LORD's lot fell, and offer it as a sin offering. But the goat on which the lot fell to be the scapegoat shall be presented alive before the LORD, to make atonement upon it, and to let it go as the scapegoat into the wilderness. . . . and Aaron shall lay both his hands on the head of the live goat, confess over it all the iniquities of the children of Israel, and all their transgressions, concerning all their sins, putting them on the head of the goat, and shall send it away into the wilderness by the hand of a suitable man. The goat shall bear on itself all their iniquities to an uninhabited land; and he shall release the goat in the wilderness.

—LEVITICUS 16:7–10, 21–22

■ . . . *Let Christ Be the Sacrifice!*

The priests always went into the first part of the tabernacle, performing the services. But into the second part the high priest went alone once a year, not without blood, which he offered for himself and for the people's sins committed in ignorance; the Holy Spirit indicating this, that the way into the Holiest of All was not yet made manifest while the first tabernacle was still standing. It was symbolic for the present time in which both gifts and sacrifices are offered which cannot make him who performed the service perfect in regard to the conscience—concerned only with foods and drinks, various washings, and fleshly ordinances imposed until the time of reformation. But Christ came as High Priest of the good things to come, with the greater and more perfect tabernacle not made with hands, that is, not of this creation. Not with the blood of goats and calves, but with His own blood He entered the Most Holy Place once for all, having obtained eternal redemption. For if the blood of bulls and goats and the ashes of a heifer, sprinkling the unclean, sanctifies for the purifying of the flesh, how much more shall the blood of Christ, who through the eternal Spirit offered Himself without spot to God, purge your conscience from dead works to serve the living God?

—HEBREWS 9:6b–14

For Christ has not entered the holy places made with hands, which are copies of the true, but into heaven itself, now to appear in the presence of God for us; not that He should offer Himself often, as the high priest enters the Most Holy Place every year with blood of another—He then would have had to suffer often since the foundation of the world; but now, once at the end of the ages, He has appeared to put away sin by the sacrifice of Himself. And as it is appointed for men to die once, but after this the judgment, so Christ was offered once to bear the sins of many. To those who eagerly wait for Him He will appear a second time, apart from sin, for salvation.

—HEBREWS 9:24–28

For it is not possible that the blood of bulls and goats could take away sins.

—HEBREWS 10:4

■ *Were You the MASCOT—Grabbing Attention? . . .*

Then He said: "A certain man had two sons. And the younger of them said to his father, 'Father, give me the portion of goods that falls to me.' So he divided to them his livelihood. And not many days after, the younger son gathered all together, journeyed to a far country, and there wasted his possessions with prodigal living. But when he had spent all, there arose a severe famine in that land, and he began to be in want. Then he went and joined himself to a citizen of that country, and he sent him into his fields to feed swine. And he would gladly have filled his stomach with the pods that the swine ate, and no one gave him anything. But when he came to himself, he said, 'How many of my father's hired servants have bread enough and to spare, and I perish with hunger! I will arise and go to my father, and will say to him, "Father, I have sinned against heaven and before you, and I am no longer worthy to be called your son. Make me like one of your hired servants."' And he arose and came to his father. But when he was still a great way off, his father saw him and had compassion, and ran and fell on his neck and kissed him. And the son said to him, 'Father, I have sinned against heaven and in your sight, and am no longer worthy to be called your son.' But the father said to his servants, 'Bring out the best robe and put it on him, and put a ring on his hand and sandals on his feet. And bring the fatted calf here and kill it, and let us eat and be merry; for this my son was dead and is alive again; he was lost and is found.' And they began to be merry."

—LUKE 15:11–24

■ . . . Or the LOST CHILD—Nice and Unnoticed?

"Now his older son was in the field. And as he came and drew near to the house, he heard music and dancing. So he called one of the servants and asked what these things meant. And he said to him, 'Your brother has come, and because he has received him safe and sound, your father has killed the fatted calf.' But he was angry and would not go in. Therefore his father came out and pleaded with him. So he answered and said to his father, 'Lo, these many years I have been serving you; I never transgressed your commandment at any time; and yet you never gave me a young goat, that I might make merry with my friends. But as soon as this son of yours came, who has devoured your livelihood with harlots, you killed the fatted calf for him.'"

—LUKE 15:25–30

■ . . . Let God Be a Loving Father to Both!

"And he said to him, 'Son, you are always with me, and all that I have is yours. It was right that we should make merry and be glad, for your brother was dead and is alive again, and was lost and is found.'"

—LUKE 15:31–32

"If you then, being evil, know how to give good gifts to your children, how much more will your

Father who is in heaven give good things to those who ask Him!"

—MATTHEW 7:11

"Are not two sparrows sold for a copper coin? And not one of them falls to the ground apart from your Father's will."

—MATTHEW 10:29

"I will be a Father to you, and you shall be My sons and daughters, says the LORD Almighty."

—2 CORINTHIANS 6:18

Behold what manner of love the Father has bestowed on us, that we should be called children of God!

—1 JOHN 3:1a

Suffering Past Abuse in the Spirit of Christ

For this is commendable, if because of conscience toward God one endures grief, suffering wrongfully. For what credit is it if, when you are beaten for your faults, you take it patiently? But when you do good and suffer for it, if you take it patiently, this is commendable before God. For to this you were called, because Christ also suffered for us, leaving us an example, that you should follow His steps: "Who committed no sin, nor was guile found in His mouth"; who, when He was reviled, did not revile in return; when He suffered, He did not threaten, but committed Himself to Him who judges righteously;

—1 PETER 2:19-23

Let this mind be in you which was also in Christ Jesus, who, being in the form of God, did not consider it robbery to be equal with God, but made Himself of no reputation, taking the form of a servant, and coming in the likeness of men. And being found in appearance as a man, He humbled Himself and became obedient to the point of death, even the death of the cross. Therefore God also has highly exalted Him and given Him the name which is above every name, that at the name of Jesus every knee should bow, of those in heaven, and of those on earth, and of those under the earth, and that every tongue should confess that Jesus Christ is Lord, to the glory of God the Father. Therefore, my beloved, as you have always obeyed, not as in my presence only, but now much more in my absence, work out your own salvation with fear and trembling; for it is God who works in you both to will and to do for His good pleasure. Do all things without murmuring and disputing, that you may become blameless and harmless, children of God without fault in the midst of a crooked and perverse generation, among whom you shine as lights in the world, holding fast the word of life, so that I may rejoice in the day of Christ that I have not run in vain or labored in vain.

—PHILIPPIANS 2:5–16

Forgiving Past Abusive Relationships

"For if you forgive men their trespasses, your heavenly Father will also forgive you. But if you do not forgive men their trespasses, neither will your Father forgive your trespasses."

—MATTHEW 6:14–15

Then Peter came to Him and said, "Lord, how often shall my brother sin against me, and I forgive him? Up to seven times?" Jesus said to him, "I do not say to you, up to seven times, but up to seventy times seven. Therefore the kingdom of heaven is like a certain king who wanted to settle accounts with his servants. And when he had begun to settle accounts, one was brought to him who owed him ten thousand talents. But as he was not able to pay, his master commanded that he be sold, with his wife and children and all that he had, and that payment be made. The servant therefore fell down before him, saying, 'Master, have patience with me, and I will pay you all.' Then the master of that servant was moved with compassion, released him, and forgave him the debt. But that servant went out and found one of his fellow servants who owed him a hundred denarii; and he laid hands on him and took him by the throat, saying, 'Pay me what you owe!' So his fellow servant fell down at his feet and begged him, saying, 'Have patience with me, and I will pay you all.' And he would not, but went and threw him into prison till he should pay the debt. So when his fellow servants saw what had been done, they were very grieved, and came and told their master all that had been done. Then his master, after he had called him, said to him, 'You wicked servant! I forgave you all that debt because you begged me. Should you not also have had compassion on your fellow servant, just as I had pity on you?' And his master was angry, and delivered him to the torturers until he should pay all that was due to him. So My heavenly Father also will do to you if each of you, from his heart, does not forgive his brother his trespasses."

—MATTHEW 18:21–35

3

Breaking the Addiction Cycle

Addiction really is a cycle, with five steps that keep taking us round and round in a downward spiral: 1) Pain, love hunger, and low self-esteem; 2) addictive agent; 3) pain relief, anesthesia; 4) consequences, relationship pain; 5) guilt and shame. The last step leads right back into the first one, fueling our "need" for more of the addictive agent. Many who have experienced this devastating cycle have echoed the words of the apostle Paul in the New Testament: "O wretched man that I am! Who will deliver me . . . ?" (Rom. 7:24).

That is the key, isn't it? Deliverance. Breaking the cycle before it can start again. And keeping it broken.

The Scriptures can help. They point to reasons for the hope that lifted Paul out of his own despair. They call us to recognize our inability to fight with willpower alone. They offer us a new way of dependence on a God who knows

all about our weaknesses but who still refuses
to turn away.

––––––––––––■––––––––––––

Recognize the Bad Effects of Addictive Agents

■ *Unfulfilled Cravings and Desires*

Now the mixed multitude who were among
them yielded to intense craving. . . .

[So] a wind went out from the LORD, and it
brought quail from the sea and left them fluttering
near the camp, about a day's journey on this side
and about a day's journey on the other side, all
around the camp, and about two cubits above the
surface of the ground.

And the people stayed up all that day, all that
night, and all the next day, and gathered the quail
(he who gathered least gathered ten homers); and
they spread them out for themselves all around
the camp.

But while the meat was still between their teeth,
before it was chewed, the wrath of the LORD was
aroused against the people, and the LORD struck
the people with a very great plague.

So he called the name of that place Kibroth Hat-
taavah, because there they buried the people who
had yielded to craving.

—NUMBERS 11:4, 31–34

It shall even be as when a hungry man
  dreams,

And look—he eats;
But he awakes, and his soul is still empty;
Or as when a thirsty man dreams,
And look—he drinks;
But he awakes, and indeed he is faint,
And his soul still craves.

—ISAIAH 29:8a

Woe is me!
For I am like those who gather summer fruits,
Like those who glean vintage grapes;
There is no cluster to eat
Of the first-ripe fruit which my soul desires.

—MICAH 7:1

■ Feeling Invincible: I Can Handle It

"Because your heart is lifted up,
And you say, 'I am a god,
I sit in the seat of gods,
In the midst of the seas,'
Yet you are a man, and not a god,
Though you set your heart as the heart of a
    god . . .
(With your wisdom and your understanding
You have gained riches for yourself,
And gathered gold and silver into your
    treasuries;
By your great wisdom in trade you have
    increased your riches,
And your heart is lifted up because of your
    riches),"

Therefore thus says the Lord GOD:
"Because you have set your heart as the heart
of a god,
Behold, therefore, I will bring strangers
against you,
The most terrible of the nations;
And they shall draw their swords against the
beauty of your wisdom,
And defile your splendor.
They shall throw you down into the Pit,
And you shall die the death of the slain
In the midst of the seas.
Will you still say before him who slays you, 'I
am a god'?
But you shall be a man, and not a god,
In the hand of him who slays you."
—EZEKIEL 28:2b, 4–9

■ *The Power of Addiction to Lead Me Astray*

Let no one say when he is tempted, "I am
tempted by God"; for God cannot be tempted by
evil, nor does He Himself tempt anyone. But each
one is tempted when he is drawn away by his own
desires and enticed. Then, when desire has conceived, it gives birth to sin; and sin, when it is full-
grown, brings forth death. Do not be deceived,
my beloved brethren. . . . Therefore lay aside all
filthiness and overflow of wickedness, and receive
with meekness the implanted word, which is able
to save your souls. . . . Pure and undefiled religion
before God and the Father is this: to visit orphans

and widows in their trouble, and to keep oneself
unspotted from the world.

—JAMES 1:13–16, 21, 27

Where do wars and fights come from among
you? Do they not come from your desires for pleasure that war in your members? . . . Or do you
think that the Scripture says in vain, "The Spirit
who dwells in us yearns jealously"? . . . Draw near
to God and He will draw near to you. Cleanse
your hands, you sinners; and purify your hearts,
you double-minded. Lament and mourn and
weep! Let your laughter be turned to mourning
and your joy to gloom. Humble yourselves in the
sight of the Lord, and He will lift you up. . . . But
now you boast in your arrogance. All such boasting is evil. Therefore, to him who knows to do
good and does not do it, to him it is sin.

—JAMES 4:1, 5, 8–10, 16–17

■ The Bad Consequences of Addictive Behaviors

Whoever has no rule over his own spirit
Is like a city broken down, without walls.

—PROVERBS 25:28

Who has woe?
Who has sorrow?
Who has contentions?
Who has complaints?
Who has wounds without cause?

Who has redness of eyes?
Those who linger long at the wine,
Those who go in search of mixed wine.
Do not look on the wine when it is red,
When it sparkles in the cup,
When it swirls around smoothly;
At the last it bites like a serpent,
And stings like a viper.
Your eyes will see strange things,
And your heart will utter perverse things.
Yes, you will be like one who lies down in the
    midst of the sea,
Or like one who lies at the top of the mast,
    saying:
"They have struck me, but I was not hurt;
They have beaten me, but I did not feel it.
When shall I awake, that I may seek another
    drink?"

—PROVERBS 23:29–35

Respond Vigorously

■ *Beware of Dulled Alertness!*

And the disciples came and said to Him, "Why
do You speak to them in parables?" He answered
and said to them, "Because it has been given to
you to know the mysteries of the kingdom of
heaven, but to them it has not been given. For
whoever has, to him more will be given, and he
will have abundance; but whoever does not have,

even what he has will be taken away from him. Therefore I speak to them in parables, because seeing they do not see, and hearing they do not hear, nor do they understand. And in them the prophecy of Isaiah is fulfilled, which says:

'Hearing you will hear and shall not
    understand,
And seeing you will see and not perceive;
For the heart of this people have grown dull.
Their ears are hard of hearing,
And their eyes they have closed,
Lest they should see with their eyes and hear
    with their ears, Lest they should understand
    with their hearts and turn,
So that I should heal them.'
But blessed are your eyes for they see, and
    your ears for they hear."

—MATTHEW 13:10-16

"Heaven and earth will pass away, but My words will by no means pass away. But take heed to yourselves, lest your hearts be weighed down with carousing, drunkenness, and cares of this life, and that Day come on you unexpectedly. For it will come as a snare on all those who dwell on the face of the whole earth."

—LUKE 21:33-35

■ Run Away!

[His master] left all that he had in Joseph's hand, and he did not know what he had except for

the bread which he ate. And Joseph was hand-
some in form and appearance. Now it came to
pass after these things that his master's wife cast
longing eyes on Joseph, and she said, "Lie with
me." But he refused and said to his master's wife,
"Look, my master does not know what is with me
in the house, and he has committed all that he has
to my hand. There is no one greater in this house
than I, nor has he kept back anything from me but
you, because you are his wife. How then can I do
this great wickedness, and sin against God?" So it
was, as she spoke to Joseph day by day, that he did
not heed her, to lie with her or to be with her. But it
happened about this time, when Joseph went into
the house to do his work, and none of the men of
the house was inside, that she caught him by his
garment, saying, "Lie with me." But he left his
garment in her hand, and fled and ran outside.

—GENESIS 39:6–12

And you, by all means keep yourselves from the
accursed things, lest you become accursed when
you take of the accursed things, and make the
camp of Israel a curse, and trouble it.

—JOSHUA 6:18

Abstain from every form of evil.

—1 THESSALONIANS 5:22

Beloved, I beg you as sojourners and pilgrims,
abstain from fleshly lusts which war against the
soul.

—1 PETER 2:11

■ *Watch!*

"But as the days of Noah were, so also will the coming of the Son of Man be. For as in the days before the flood, they were eating and drinking, marrying and giving in marriage, until the day that Noah entered the ark, and did not know until the flood came and took them all away, so also will the coming of the Son of Man be. Then two men will be in the field: one will be taken and the other left. Two women will be grinding at the mill: one will be taken and the other left. Watch therefore, for you do not know what hour your Lord is coming."

—MATTHEW 24:37–42

"Take heed, watch and pray; for you do not know when the time is. It is like a man going to a far country, who left his house and gave authority to his servants, and to each his work, and commanded the doorkeeper to watch. Watch therefore, for you do not know when the master of the house is coming—in the evening, at midnight, at the crowing of the rooster, or in the morning—lest, coming suddenly, he find you sleeping. And what I say to you, I say to all: Watch!"

—MARK 13:33–37

Watch, stand fast in the faith, be brave, be strong.

—1 CORINTHIANS 16:13

Praying always with all prayer and supplication in the Spirit, being watchful to this end with all perseverance and supplication for all the saints

—EPHESIANS 6:18

Therefore let us not sleep, as others do, but let us watch and be sober.

—1 THESSALONIANS 5:6

Look to God for Help

■ *God Has Desires, Too: For Us!*

[God] desires all men to be saved and to come to the knowledge of the truth. For there is one God and one Mediator between God and men, the Man Christ Jesus, who gave Himself a ransom for all.

—1 TIMOTHY 2:4–6a

"And as Moses lifted up the serpent in the wilderness, even so must the Son of Man be lifted up, that whoever believes in Him should not perish but have eternal life. For God so loved the world that He gave His only begotten Son, that whoever believes in Him should not perish but have everlasting life. For God did not send His Son into the world to condemn the world, but that the world through Him might be saved."

—JOHN 3:14–17

And the Spirit and the bride say, "Come!" And
let him who hears say, "Come!" And let him who
thirsts come. And whoever desires, let him take
the water of life freely.

—REVELATION 22:17

■ *God Fulfills Our Desires*

Do not fret because of evildoers,
Nor be envious of the workers of iniquity.
For they shall soon be cut down like the grass,
And wither as the green herb.
Trust in the LORD, and do good;
Dwell in the land, and feed on His
  faithfulness.
Delight yourself also in the LORD,
And He shall give you the desires of your
  heart. . . .
A little that a righteous man has
Is better than the riches of many wicked. . . .
The LORD knows the days of the upright,
And their inheritance shall be forever.
They shall not be ashamed in the evil time,
And in the days of famine they shall be
  satisfied. . . .
The steps of a good man are ordered by the
  LORD,
And He delights in his way. . . .
He is ever merciful, and lends;
And his descendants are blessed.
Depart from evil, and do good;

And dwell forevermore. . . .
But the salvation of the righteous is from the
    LORD;
He is their strength in the time of trouble.
                    —PSALM 37:1–4, 16, 18–19, 23, 26–27, 39

■ God Comforts, Loves, and Protects

The LORD is my shepherd; I shall not want.
He makes me to lie down in green pastures;
He leads me beside the still waters.
He restores my soul;
He leads me in the paths of righteousness
For His name's sake.
Yea, though I walk through the valley of the
    shadow of death, I will fear no evil;
For You are with me; Your rod and Your staff,
    they comfort me.
You prepare a table before me in the presence
    of my enemies;
You anoint my head with oil; My cup runs
    over.
Surely goodness and mercy shall follow me
All the days of my life;
And I will dwell in the house of the LORD
Forever.
                                            —PSALM 23

Blessed be the God and Father of our Lord Jesus
Christ, the Father of mercies and God of all comfort, who comforts us in all our tribulation, that we
may be able to comfort those who are in any trou-

ble, with the comfort with which we ourselves are
comforted by God.

—2 CORINTHIANS 1:3-4

HEAR my cry, O God;
Attend to my prayer.
From the end of the earth I will cry to You,
When my heart is overwhelmed;
Lead me to the rock that is higher than I.
For You have been a shelter for me,
A strong tower from the enemy.
I will abide in Your tabernacle forever;
I will trust in the shelter of Your wings.

—PSALM 61:1-4

My soul, wait silently for God alone,
For my expectation is from Him.
He only is my rock and my salvation;
He is my defense; I shall not be moved.
In God is my salvation and my glory;
The rock of my strength,
And my refuge, is in God.

—PSALM 62:5-7

He who dwells in the secret place of the Most
    High
Shall abide under the shadow of the Almighty.
I will say of the LORD, "He is my refuge and
    my fortress;
My God, in Him I will trust."
Surely He shall deliver you from the snare of
    the fowler

And from the perilous pestilence.
He shall cover you with His feathers,
And under His wings you shall take refuge;
His truth shall be your shield and buckler.

—PSALM 91:1-4

Saying Good-bye

What is your relationship with your parents at the moment (whether they are still living or not)? As you think about your motivations for the things you do in your life, how much of your activity is determined by a need for approval from your parents? Or how much of your security still depends on being closely tied to home? Or what self-expectations still prod you from old parental "tapes" that keep playing in the back of your mind?

Tough questions! But they lead us to the task that every adult who truly wants to be emotionally healthy and addiction-free must accomplish: cutting the apron strings for good and saying goodbye. Naturally, we will maintain a relationship with our parents. We never stop being a son or a daughter, even after our parents are gone. But we can learn to relate to them as adults, no longer as the children we once were. By offering ourselves to our parents as healthy adults, we can expand the relationship and watch it blossom in new and unpredictable ways. We overcome the old ruts. New vistas of mutual self-discovery open before us. Exciting!

Leaving Old Values

■ *Turning Away from the World's Values*

Do not love the world or the things in the world. If anyone loves the world, the love of the Father is not in him. For all that is in the world—the lust of the flesh, the lust of the eyes, and the pride of life—is not of the Father but is of the world. And the world is passing away, and the lust of it; but he who does the will of God abides forever.

—1 JOHN 2:15–17

For whatever is born of God overcomes the world. And this is the victory that has overcome the world—our faith. Who is he who overcomes the world, but he who believes that Jesus is the Son of God?

—1 JOHN 5:4–5

■ *Letting Go of the Worthless Things in Life*

Remove from me the way of lying,
And grant me Your law graciously.
I have chosen the way of truth;

Your judgments I have laid before me.
I cling to Your testimonies;
O Lord, do not put me to shame!
I will run in the way of Your commandments,
For You shall enlarge my heart.
Teach me, O Lord, the way of Your statutes,
And I shall keep it to the end.
Give me understanding, and I shall keep Your
　　law;
Indeed, I shall observe it with my whole
　　heart.
Make me walk in the path of Your
　　commandments,
For I delight in it.
Incline my heart to Your testimonies,
And not to covetousness.
Turn away my eyes from looking at worthless
　　things,
And revive me in Your way.

—PSALM 119:29–37

■ *Letting Go of Earthly Life to Gain Eternal Life*

But Jesus answered them, saying, "The hour has come that the Son of Man should be glorified. Most assuredly, I say to you, unless a grain of wheat falls into the ground and dies, it remains alone; but if it dies, it produces much grain. He who loves his life will lose it, and he who hates his life in this world will keep it for eternal life. If anyone serves Me, let him follow Me; and where I am, there My servant will be also. If anyone serves Me, him My Father will honor."

—JOHN 12:23–26

Leaving Old Securities

■ *Departing from Father and Mother*

And the LORD God caused a deep sleep to fall on Adam, and he slept; and He took one of his ribs, and closed up the flesh in its place. Then the rib which the LORD God had taken from man He made into a woman, and He brought her to the man. And Adam said:

"This is now bone of my bones
And flesh of my flesh;
She shall be called Woman,
Because she was taken out of Man."
Therefore a man shall leave his father and
    mother and be joined to his wife, and they
    shall become one flesh.

—GENESIS 2:21–24

Now after John was put in prison, Jesus came to Galilee, preaching the gospel of the kingdom of God, and saying, "The time is fulfilled, and the kingdom of God is at hand. Repent, and believe in the gospel." And as He walked by the Sea of Galilee, He saw Simon and Andrew his brother casting a net into the sea; for they were fishermen. Then Jesus said to them, "Come after Me, and I will make you become fishers of men." And immediately they left their nets and followed Him. When He had gone a little farther from there, He saw James the son of Zebedee, and John his brother, who also were in the boat mending their nets. And immediately He called them, and they left their father Zebedee in the boat with the hired servants, and went after Him.

—MARK 1:14–20

■ 'Leaving' Home and Family of Origin

Now it happened as they journeyed on the road, that someone said to Him, "Lord, I will follow You wherever You go." And Jesus said to him, "Foxes have holes and birds of the air have nests, but the Son of Man has nowhere to lay His head." Then He said to another, "Follow Me." But he said, "Lord, let me first go and bury my father." Jesus said to him, "Let the dead bury their own dead, but you go and preach the kingdom of God."

—LUKE 9:57–60

Then He said to him, "A certain man gave a great supper and invited many, and sent his servant at supper time to say to those who were invited, 'Come, for all things are now ready.' But they all with one accord began to make excuses. The first said to him, 'I have bought a piece of ground, and I must go and see it. I ask you to have me excused.' And another said, 'I have bought five yoke of oxen, and I am going to test them. I ask you to have me excused.' Still another said, 'I have married a wife, and therefore I cannot come.' So that servant came and reported these things to his master. Then the master of the house, being angry, said to his servant, 'Go out quickly into the streets and lanes of the city, and bring in here the poor and the maimed and the lame and the blind.' And the servant said, 'Master, it is done as you commanded, and still there is room.' Then the master said to the servant, 'Go out into the highways and hedges, and compel them to come in, that my house may be filled. For I say to you that none of those men who were invited shall taste my supper.'" Now great multitudes went with Him. And He turned and said to them, "If anyone comes to Me and does not hate his father and mother, wife and children, brothers and sisters, yes, and his own life also, he cannot be My disciple. And whoever does not bear his cross and come after Me cannot be My disciple. For which of you, intending to build a tower, does not sit down first and count the cost, whether he has enough to finish it—lest, after he has laid the foundation, and is not able to finish it, all who see it begin to mock him, saying, 'This man began to build and was not able to finish.' Or what king, going to make war against another king, does not sit down first and consider whether he is able with ten thousand to meet him who comes against him with twenty thousand? Or else, while the other is still a great way off, he sends a delegation and asks conditions of peace. So likewise, whoever of you does not forsake all that he has cannot be My disciple."

—LUKE 14:16–33

■ Focusing on Our True Home: Heaven

For we know that if our earthly house, this tent, is destroyed, we have a building from God, a house not made with hands, eternal in the heavens. For in this we groan, earnestly desiring to be clothed with our habitation which is from heaven, if indeed, having been clothed, we shall not be found naked. For we who are in this tent groan, being burdened, not because we want to be unclothed, but further clothed, that mortality may be swallowed up by life. Now He who has prepared us for this very thing is God, who also has given us the Spirit as a guarantee. Therefore we are always confident, knowing that while we are at home in the body we are absent from the Lord.

—2 CORINTHIANS 5:1–6

And I saw a new heaven and a new earth, for the first heaven and the first earth had passed away. Also there was no more sea. Then I, John, saw the holy city, New Jerusalem, coming down out of heaven from God, prepared as a bride adorned for her husband. And I heard a loud voice from heaven saying, "Behold, the tabernacle of God is with men, and He will dwell with them, and they shall be His people and God Himself will be with them and be their God. And God will wipe away every tear from their eyes; there shall be no more death, nor sorrow, nor crying; and there shall be no more pain, for the former things have passed away."

—REVELATION 21:1-4

And the city is laid out as a square; its length is as great as its breadth. And he measured the city with the reed: twelve thousand furlongs. Its length, breadth, and height are equal. Then he measured its wall: one hundred and forty-four cubits, according to the measure of a man, that is, of an angel. And the construction of its wall was of jasper; and the city was pure gold, like clear glass. And the foundations of the wall of the city were adorned with all kinds of precious stones: the first foundation was jasper, the second sapphire, the third chalcedony, the fourth emerald, the fifth sardonyx, the sixth sardius, the seventh chrysolite, the eighth beryl, the ninth topaz, the tenth chrysoprase, the eleventh jacinth, and the twelfth amethyst. And the twelve gates were twelve pearls: each individual gate was of one pearl. And the street of the city was pure gold, like transparent glass. But I saw no temple in it, for the Lord God Almighty and the Lamb are its temple. And the city had no need of the sun or of the moon to shine in it, for the glory of God illuminated it, and the Lamb is its light. And the nations of those who are saved shall walk in its light, and the kings of the earth bring their glory and honor into it. Its gates shall not be shut at all by day (there shall be no night there). And they shall bring the glory and the honor of the nations into it. But there shall by no means enter it anything that defiles, or causes an abomination or a lie, but only those who are written in the Lamb's Book of Life.

—REVELATION 21:16–27

■ *Resting in God*

"Come to Me, all you who labor and are heavy laden, and I will give you rest. Take My yoke upon you and learn from Me, for I am gentle and lowly in heart, and you will find rest for your souls. For My yoke is easy and My burden is light."

—MATTHEW 11:28–30

Therefore, since a promise remains of entering His rest, let us fear lest any of you seem to have come short of it. For indeed the gospel was preached to us as well as to them; but the word which they heard did not profit them, not being mixed with faith in those who heard it. . . . Since therefore it remains that some must enter it, and those to whom it was first preached did not enter because of disobedience. . . . There remains therefore a rest for the people of God. For he who has entered His rest has himself also ceased from his works as God did from His. Let us therefore be diligent to enter that rest. . . .

—HEBREWS 4:1–2, 6, 9–11a

Leaving Old Sources of Approval

■ *Seeking to Please God, not Other Humans*

"Did we not strictly command you not to teach in this name? And look, you have filled Jerusalem with your doctrine, and intend to bring this Man's blood on us!" Then Peter and the other apostles answered and said: "We ought to obey God rather than men."

—ACTS 5:28–29

For those who live according to the flesh set their minds on the things of the flesh, but those who live according to the Spirit, the things of the Spirit. For to be carnally minded is death, but to be spiritually minded is life and peace. Because the carnal mind is enmity against God; for it is not subject to the law of God, nor indeed can be. So then, those who are in the flesh cannot please God.

—ROMANS 8:5–8

But as we have been approved by God to be entrusted with the gospel, even so we speak, not as pleasing men, but God who tests our hearts.

—1 THESSALONIANS 2:4

■ *Meeting New, Divine Expectations*

And God spoke all these words, saying: "I am the LORD your God, who brought you out of the land of Egypt, out of the house of bondage.

"You shall have no other gods before Me.

"You shall not make for yourself any carved image, or any likeness of anything that is in heaven above, or that is in the earth beneath, or that is in the water under the earth; you shall not bow down to them nor serve them. For I, the LORD your God, am a jealous God, visiting the iniquity of the fathers on the children to the third and fourth generations of those who hate Me, but showing mercy to thousands, to those who love Me and keep My commandments.

"You shall not take the name of the LORD your God in vain, for the LORD will not hold him guiltless who takes His name in vain.

"Remember the Sabbath day, to keep it holy. Six days you shall labor and do all your work, but the seventh day is the Sabbath of the LORD your God. In it you shall do no work: you, nor your son, nor your daughter, nor your manservant, nor your maidservant, nor your cattle, nor your stranger who is within your gates. For in six days the LORD made the heavens and the earth, the sea, and all that is in them, and rested the seventh day. Therefore the LORD blessed the Sabbath day and hallowed it.

"Honor your father and your mother, that your days may be long upon the land which the LORD your God is giving you.

"You shall not murder.

"You shall not commit adultery.

"You shall not steal.

"You shall not bear false witness against your neighbor.

"You shall not covet your neighbor's house; you shall not covet your neighbor's wife, nor his man-servant, nor his maidservant, nor his ox, nor his donkey, nor anything that is your neighbor's."

—EXODUS 20:1–17

For we dare not class ourselves or compare ourselves with those who commend themselves. But they, measuring themselves by themselves, and comparing themselves among themselves, are not wise. We, however, will not boast beyond measure, but within the limits of the sphere which God appointed us—a sphere which especially includes you. For we are not extending ourselves beyond our sphere (thus not reaching you), for it was to you that we came with the gospel of Christ; not boasting of things beyond measure, that is, in other men's labors, but having hope, that as your faith is increased, we shall be greatly enlarged by you in our sphere, to preach the gospel in the regions beyond you, and not to boast in another man's sphere of accomplishment. But "He who glories, let him glory in the LORD." For not he who commends himself is approved, but whom the Lord commends.

—2 CORINTHIANS 10:12–18

CHAPTER 5

Experiencing Grief

Those with chemical dependencies have experienced losses of all kinds. We're not just talking about family members who have died, though those are certainly significant losses. But consider a pre-teen son, for example, whose father dies. The boy experiences not only the death of his father, but the death of his own childhood, as well. As he begins to "take care of" his mother (as well-meaning relatives at the funeral told him to do), he becomes quite serious about the insecurities of life. Perhaps he begins to think more as an adult, burdened with responsibilities, than as a child who should be out playing sandlot football. Many of us need to grieve the loss of our childhoods!

Can you identify your own personal losses? Make a list and meditate on what you have had to give up in your life. Having had to let go of all those things brings grief. And now, in your recovery process, you are called upon to give up yet another significant thing: the "benefits" of addiction—the pain relief, anesthesia, temporary escape from real problems. We must allow ourselves to express the emotions that flow from such profound losses. Crying is definitely in order here, for as long as it takes . . . over the years of recovery grieving.

Feel the Desolation of Loss

■ *Grieving, Rather than Anesthesizing with Addictive Agents*

"Oh, that my grief were fully weighed,
And my calamity laid with it on the balances!"
—JOB 6:2

"Though I speak, my grief is not relieved;
And if I remain silent, how am I eased?"
—JOB 16:6

My eye wastes away because of grief;
It grows old because of all my enemies.
—PSALM 6:7

■ *Grieving Over Past Sin*

When these things were done, the leaders came to me, saying, "The people of Israel and the priests and the Levites have not separated themselves from the peoples of the lands, with respect to the abominations of the Canaanites. . . ." So when I heard this thing, I tore my garment and my robe, and plucked out some of the hair of my head and beard, and sat down astonished. Then everyone who trembled at the words of the God of Israel assembled to me, because of the transgression of those who had been carried away captive, and I sat astonished until the evening sacrifice. At the evening sacrifice I arose from my fasting; and having torn my garment and my robe, I fell on my knees and spread out my hands to the LORD my God, and said: "O my God, I am too ashamed and humiliated to lift up my face to You, my God; for our iniquities have risen higher than our heads, and our guilt has grown up to the heavens. . . . And now, O our God, what shall we say after this? For we have forsaken Your commandments. . . . O LORD God of Israel, You are righteous, for we are left as a remnant, as it is this day. Here we are before You, in our guilt, though no one can stand before You because of this!"

—EZRA 9:1a, 3–6, 10, 15

■ Grieving Over Past Sexual Abuse

And David sent home to Tamar, saying, "Now go to your brother Amnon's house, and prepare food for him." So Tamar went to her brother Amnon's house; and he was lying down. Then she took flour and kneaded it, made cakes in his sight, and baked the cakes. And she took the pan and placed them out before him, but he refused to eat.

Then Amnon said, "Have everyone go out from me." And they all went out from him. Then Amnon said to Tamar, "Bring the food into the bedroom, that I may eat from your hand." And Tamar took the cakes which she had made, and brought them to Amnon her brother in the bedroom. Now when she had brought them to him to eat, he took hold of her and said to her, "Come, lie with me, my sister." And she answered him, "No, my brother, do not force me, for no such thing should be done in Israel. Do not do this disgraceful thing! And I, where could I take my shame? . . ." However, he would not heed her voice; and being stronger than she, he forced her and lay with her. . . . Then he called his servant who attended him, and said, "Here! Put this woman out, away from me, and bolt the door behind her." Now she had on a robe of many colors, for the king's virgin daughters wore such apparel. And his servant put her out and bolted the door behind her. Then Tamar put ashes on her head, and tore her robe of many colors that was on her, and laid her hand on her head and went away crying bitterly.

—2 SAMUEL 13:7–14, 17–19

■ Grieving Over Past Failure

Now when they had kindled a fire in the midst of the courtyard and sat down together, Peter sat among them. And a certain servant girl, seeing him as he sat by the fire, looked intently at him and said, "This man was also with Him." But he denied Him, saying, "Woman, I do not know Him." And after a little while another saw him and said, "You also are of them." But Peter said, "Man, I am not!" Then after about an hour had passed, another confidently affirmed, saying, "Surely this fellow also was with Him, for he is a Galilean." But Peter said, "Man, I do not know what you are saying!" And immediately, while he was still speaking, the rooster crowed. And the Lord turned and looked at Peter. And Peter remembered the word of the Lord, how He had said to him, "Before the rooster crows, you will deny Me three times." Then Peter went out and wept bitterly.

—LUKE 22:55–62

Accept God's Consolation in Despair

■ *Job Loses Everything . . .*

Now there was a day when his sons and daughters were eating and drinking wine in their oldest brother's house; and a messenger came to Job and said, "The oxen were plowing and the donkeys feeding beside them, when the Sabeans raided them and took them away—indeed they have killed the servants with the edge of the sword; and I alone have escaped to tell you!" While he was still speaking, another also came and said, "The fire of God fell from heaven and burned up the sheep and the servants, and consumed them; and I alone have escaped to tell you!" While he was still speaking, another also came and said, "The Chaldeans formed three bands, raided the camels and took them away, yes, and killed the servants with the edge of the sword; and I alone have escaped to tell you!" While he was still speaking, another also came and said, "Your sons and daughters were eating and drinking wine in their oldest brother's house, and suddenly a great wind came from across the wilderness and struck the four corners of the house, and it fell on the young men, and they are dead; and I alone have escaped to tell you!" Then Job arose and tore his robe and shaved his head; and he fell to the ground and worshiped. And he said:

"Naked I came from my mother's womb,
And naked shall I return there.
The LORD gave, and the LORD has taken away;
Blessed be the name of the LORD."

—JOB 1:13–21

■ . . . *But Gets Twice as Much Back*

And the LORD restored Job's losses when he prayed for his friends. Indeed the LORD gave Job twice as much as he had before. Then all his brothers, all his sisters, and all those who had been his acquaintances before, came to him and ate food with him in his house; and they consoled him and comforted him for all the adversity that the LORD had brought upon him. Each one gave him a piece of silver and each a ring of gold. Now the LORD

blessed the latter days of Job more than his beginning; for he had fourteen thousand sheep, six
thousand camels, one thousand yoke of oxen, and
one thousand female donkeys. He also had seven
sons and three daughters. And he called the name
of the first Jemimah, the name of the second Ke-
ziah, and the name of the third Keren-Happuch.
In all the land were found no women so beautiful
as the daughters of Job; and their father gave them
an inheritance among their brothers. After this Job
lived one hundred and forty years, and saw his
children and grandchildren for four generations.
So Job died, old and full of days.

—JOB 42:10–17

■ *God Saves Us from Despair*

I will extol You, O LORD, for You have lifted
    me up,
And have not let my foes rejoice over me.
O LORD my God, I cried out to You,
And You have healed me.
O LORD, You have brought my soul up from
    the grave;
You have kept me alive, that I should not go
    down to the pit.
Sing praise to the LORD,
You saints of His,
And give thanks at the remembrance of His
    holy name.
For His anger is but for a moment,
His favor is for life;

Weeping may endure for a night,
But joy comes in the morning.

—PSALM 30:1–5

For the grace of God that brings salvation has appeared to all men, teaching us that, denying ungodliness and worldly lusts, we should live soberly, righteously, and godly in the present age, looking for the blessed hope and glorious appearing of our great God and Savior Jesus Christ, who gave Himself for us, that He might redeem us from every lawless deed and purify for Himself His own special people, zealous for good works.

—TITUS 2:11–14

We are hard pressed on every side, yet not crushed; we are perplexed, but not in despair; persecuted, but not forsaken; struck down, but not destroyed. . . . knowing that He who raised up the Lord Jesus will also raise us up with Jesus, and will present us with you. . . . Therefore we do not lose heart. Even though our outward man is perishing, yet the inward man is being renewed day by day. For our light affliction, which is but for a moment, is working for us a far more exceeding and eternal weight of glory, while we do not look at the things which are seen, but at the things which are not seen. For the things which are seen are temporary, but the things which are not seen are eternal.

—2 CORINTHIANS 4:8–9, 14, 16–18

■ Grief and Sorrow Will Be No More

Strengthen the weak hands,
And make firm the feeble knees.
Say to those who are fearful-hearted,
"Be strong, do not fear!
Behold, your God will come with vengeance,
With the recompense of God;
He will come and save you."
Then the eyes of the blind shall be opened,
And the ears of the deaf shall be unstopped.
Then the lame shall leap like a deer,
And the tongue of the dumb sing.
For waters shall burst forth in the wilderness,
And streams in the desert.
The parched ground shall become a pool,
And the thirsty land springs of water;
In the habitation of jackals, where each lay,
There shall be grass with reeds and rushes.
A highway shall be there, and a road,
And it shall be called the Highway of
     Holiness.
The unclean shall not pass over it,
But it shall be for others.
Whoever walks the road, although a fool,
Shall not go astray.
No lion shall be there,
Nor shall any ravenous beast go up on it;
It shall not be found there.
But the redeemed shall walk there,
And the ransomed of the LORD shall return,

And come to Zion with singing,
With everlasting joy on their heads.
They shall obtain joy and gladness,
And sorrow and sighing shall flee away.

—ISAIAH 35:3–10

After these things I looked, and behold, a great multitude which no one could number, of all nations, tribes, peoples, and tongues, standing before the throne and before the Lamb, clothed with white robes, with palm branches in their hands, and crying out with a loud voice, saying, "Salvation belongs to our God who sits on the throne, and to the Lamb!" And all the angels stood around the throne and the elders and the four living creatures, and fell on their faces before the throne and worshiped God, saying:

"Amen! Blessing and glory and wisdom,
Thanksgiving and honor and power and
    might,
Be to our God forever and ever.
Amen."

Then one of the elders answered, saying to me, "Who are these arrayed in white robes, and where did they come from?" And I said to him, "Sir, you know." So he said to me, "These are the ones who come out of the great tribulation, and washed their robes and made them white in the blood of the Lamb. Therefore they are before the throne of God, and serve Him day and night in His temple.

And He who sits on the throne will dwell among them. They shall neither hunger anymore nor thirst anymore; the sun shall not strike them, nor any heat; for the Lamb who is in the midst of the throne will shepherd them and lead them to living fountains of waters. And God will wipe away every tear from their eyes."

—REVELATION 7:9–17

Cling to the Ultimate Solution to Grief

■ *Death Will Be Destroyed!*

For I delivered to you first of all that which I also received: that Christ died for our sins according to the Scriptures, and that He was buried, and that He rose again the third day according to the Scriptures. . . . Now if Christ is preached that He has been raised from the dead, how do some among you say that there is no resurrection of the dead? But if there is no resurrection of the dead, then Christ is not risen. And if Christ is not risen, then our preaching is vain and your faith is also vain. Yes, and we are found false witnesses of God, because we have testified of God that He raised up Christ, whom He did not raise up—if in fact the dead do not rise. For if the dead do not rise, then Christ is not risen. And if Christ is not risen, your faith is futile; you are still in your sins! Then also those who have fallen asleep in Christ have perished. If in this life only we have hope in Christ, we are of all men the most pitiable. But now Christ is risen from the dead, and has become the firstfruits of those who have fallen asleep. . . . Behold, I tell you a mystery: We shall not all sleep, but we shall all be changed—in a moment, in the twinkling of an eye, at the last trumpet. For the trumpet will sound, and the dead will be raised incorruptible, and we shall be changed. For this corruptible must put on incorruption, and this mortal must put on immortality. So when this corruptible has put on incorruption, and this mortal has put on immortality, then shall be brought to pass the saying that is written: "Death is swallowed up in victory."

"O Death, where is your sting?
O Hades, where is your victory?"
—1 CORINTHIANS 15:3–4, 12–20, 51–55

■ We Will Be Raised!

But I do not want you to be ignorant, brethren, concerning those who have fallen asleep, lest you sorrow as others who have no hope. For if we believe that Jesus died and rose again, even so God will bring with Him those who sleep in Jesus. For this we say to you by the word of the Lord, that we who are alive and remain until the coming of the Lord will by no means precede those who are asleep. For the Lord Himself will descend from heaven with a shout, with the voice of an archangel, and with the trumpet of God. And the dead in

Christ will rise first. Then we who are alive and remain shall be caught up together with them in the clouds to meet the Lord in the air. And thus we shall always be with the Lord. Therefore comfort one another with these words.

—1 THESSALONIANS 4:13–18

Developing New Self-Perceptions

"I will not make mistakes. . . . I must meet everyone's needs. . . . I can win everyone's approval. . . . I will never let anybody down. . . . No one should ever get mad at me." Is this really possible? What happens to a person who tries to maintain such a god-like approach to life?

If we have lived to this point with such impossible expectations for ourselves, it's no surprise that we may seek an escape. But we've got to change our self-perceptions! Repeat after me: I will definitely make mistakes. . . . I cannot meet all your needs. . . . I will do my best. . . . Some people will be displeased with me. . . . I am only human. . . . I am not God. Get the picture?

I Can't Let Anyone See How Bad I Really Am

I sought the LORD, and He heard me,
And delivered me from all my fears.

They looked to Him and were radiant,
And their faces were not ashamed.

—PSALM 34:4–5

Blessed is he whose transgression is forgiven,
Whose sin is covered. . . .
For this cause everyone who is godly shall
    pray to You
In a time when You may be found;
Surely in a flood of great waters
They shall not come near him.
You are my hiding place;
You shall preserve me from trouble;
You shall surround me with songs of
    deliverance.
I will instruct you and teach you in the way
    you should go;
I will guide you with My eye.

—PSALM 32:1, 6–8

I Am Unlovable

What then shall we say to these things? If God is
for us, who can be against us? He who did not
spare His own Son, but delivered Him up for us
all, how shall He not with Him also freely give us
all things? Who shall bring a charge against God's
elect? It is God who justifies. Who is he who con-
demns? It is Christ who died, and furthermore is
also risen, who is even at the right hand of God,
who also makes intercession for us. Who shall

separate us from the love of Christ? Shall tribulation, or distress, or persecution, or famine, or nakedness, or peril, or sword? As it is written: "For Your sake we are killed all day long; we are accounted as sheep for the slaughter." Yet in all these things we are more than conquerors through Him who loved us. For I am persuaded that neither death nor life, nor angels nor principalities nor powers, nor things present nor things to come, nor height nor depth, nor any other created thing, shall be able to separate us from the love of God which is in Christ Jesus our Lord.

—ROMANS 8:31-39

I Don't Matter to Anyone

Then the king said, "Is there not still someone of the house of Saul, to whom I may show the kindness of God?" And Ziba said to the king, "There is still a son of Jonathan who is lame in his feet. . . ." Now when Mephibosheth the son of Jonathan, the son of Saul, had come to David, he fell on his face and prostrated himself. Then David said, "Mephibosheth?" And he answered, "Here is your servant!" So David said to him, "Do not fear, for I will surely show you kindness for Jonathan your father's sake, and will restore to you all the land of Saul your grandfather; and you shall eat bread at my table continually." Then he bowed himself,

and said, "What is your servant, that you should
look upon such a dead dog as I?"

—2 SAMUEL 9:3, 6–8

Therefore He has mercy on whom He wills. . . .
that He might make known the riches of His glory
on the vessels of mercy, which He had prepared
beforehand for glory. . . . As He says also in Ho-
sea:

"I will call them My people, who were not My
    people,
And her beloved, who was not beloved."
"And it shall come to pass in the place where
    it was said to them,
'You are not My people,'
There they will be called sons of the living
    God."

—ROMANS 9:18a, 23, 25–26

I Can't Be Okay Unless I Have Everyone's Approval

Who has believed our report?
And to whom has the arm of the LORD been
    revealed?
For He shall grow up before Him as a tender
    plant,
And as a root out of dry ground.
He has no form or comeliness;

And when we see Him,
There is no beauty that we should desire Him.
He is despised and rejected by men,
A man of sorrows and acquainted with grief.
And we hid, as it were, our faces from Him;
He was despised, and we did not esteem
    Him.
Surely He has borne our griefs
And carried our sorrows;
Yet we esteemed Him stricken,
Smitten by God, and afflicted.
But He was wounded for our transgressions,
He was bruised for our iniquities;
The chastisement for our peace was upon
    Him,
And by His stripes we are healed.

—ISAIAH 53:1–5

"If the world hates you, you know that it hated Me before it hated you. If you were of the world, the world would love its own. Yet because you are not of the world, but I chose you out of the world, therefore the world hates you. Remember the word that I said to you, 'A servant is not greater than his master.' If they persecuted Me, they will also persecute you. If they kept My word, they will keep yours also. But all these things they will do to you for My name's sake, because they do not know Him who sent Me. If I had not come and spoken to them, they would have no sin, but now they have no excuse for their sin. He who hates Me hates My Father also. If I had not done among them the works which no one else did, they would have no sin; but now they have seen and also hated both Me and My Father. But this happened that the word might be fulfilled which is written in their law, 'They hated Me without a cause.'"

—JOHN 15:18–25

I Can Be Valuable Only If I'm Constantly Busy, Doing for Others

Now it happened as they went that He entered a certain village; and a certain woman named Martha welcomed Him into her house. And she had a sister called Mary, who also sat at Jesus' feet and heard His word. But Martha was distracted with much serving, and she approached Him and said, "Lord, do You not care that my sister has left me to serve alone? Therefore tell her to help me." And Jesus answered and said to her, "Martha, Martha, you are worried and troubled about many things. But one thing is needed, and Mary has chosen that good part, which will not be taken away from her."

—LUKE 10:38–42

I Must Be Perfect!

Also He spoke this parable to some who trusted in themselves that they were righteous, and despised others: "Two men went up to the temple to pray, one a Pharisee and the other a tax collector. The Pharisee stood and prayed thus with himself, 'God, I thank You that I am not like other men— extortioners, unjust, adulterers, or even as this tax collector. I fast twice a week; I give tithes of all that I possess.' And the tax collector, standing afar off, would not so much as raise his eyes to heaven, but beat his breast, saying, 'God, be merciful to me a sinner!' I tell you, this man went down to his house justified rather than the other; for everyone who exalts himself will be abased, and he who humbles himself will be exalted."

—LUKE 18:9–14

I Can't Trust Anyone

God is not a man, that He should lie,
Nor a son of man, that He should repent.
Has He said, and will He not do?
Or has He spoken, and will He not make it good?

—NUMBERS 23:19

And the heavens will praise Your wonders, O LORD;
Your faithfulness also in the congregation of the saints.
For who in the heavens can be compared to the LORD?
Who among the sons of the mighty can be likened to the LORD?

God is greatly to be feared in the assembly of
   the saints,
And to be held in reverence by all those who
   are around Him.
O LORD God of hosts,
Who is mighty like You, O LORD?
Your faithfulness also surrounds You. . . .
My covenant I will not break,
Nor alter the word that has gone out of My
   lips.

—PSALM 89:5–8, 34

Trust in the LORD with all your heart,
And lean not on your own understanding;
In all your ways acknowledge Him,
And He shall direct your paths.

—PROVERBS 3:5–6

For what if some did not believe? Will their unbelief make the faithfulness of God without effect?
Certainly not! Indeed, let God be true but every
man a liar. . . .

—ROMANS 3:3–4a

"Surely blessing I will bless you, and multiply-
ing I will multiply you." And so, after he had patiently endured, he obtained the promise. For men
indeed swear by the greater, and an oath for con-
firmation is for them an end of all dispute. Thus
God, determining to show more abundantly to the
heirs of promise the immutability of His counsel,
confirmed it by an oath, that by two immutable

things, in which it is impossible for God to lie, we might have strong consolation, who have fled for refuge to lay hold of the hope set before us. This hope we have as an anchor of the soul, both sure and steadfast, and which enters the Presence behind the veil.

—HEBREWS 6:14–19

I Should Be Ashamed of Myself!

My dishonor is continually before me,
And the shame of my face has covered me.

—PSALM 44:15

You know my reproach, my shame, and my dishonor;
My adversaries are all before You.

—PSALM 69:19

In You, O LORD, I put my trust;
Let me never be put to shame.

—PSALM 71:1

Do not fear, for you will not be ashamed;
Nor be disgraced, for you will not be put to shame;
For you will forget the shame of your youth.

—ISAIAH 54:4a

Instead of your shame you shall have double honor,

And instead of confusion they shall rejoice in their portion. Therefore in their land they shall possess double;

Everlasting joy shall be theirs.

—ISAIAH 61:7

You shall eat in plenty and be satisfied,
And praise the name of the LORD your God,
Who has dealt wondrously with you;
And My people shall never be put to shame.
Then you shall know that I am in the midst of
    Israel,
And that I am the LORD your God
And there is no other.
My people shall never be put to shame.

—JOEL 2:26–27

As it is written:
"Behold, I lay in Zion a stumbling stone and
    rock of offense,
And whoever believes on Him will not be put
    to shame."

—ROMANS 9:33

I Can't Bear Anyone Being Angry with Me

Beloved, do not think it strange concerning the fiery trial which is to try you, as though some strange thing happened to you; but rejoice to the extent that you partake of Christ's sufferings, that when His glory is revealed, you may also be glad with exceeding joy. If you are reproached for the name of Christ, blessed are you, for the Spirit of glory and of God rests upon you. On their part He is blasphemed, but on your part He is glorified. But let none of you suffer as a murderer, a thief, an evildoer, or as a busybody in other people's matters. Yet if anyone suffers as a Christian, let him not be ashamed, but let him glorify God in this matter. For the time has come for judgment to begin at the house of God; and if it begins with us first, what will be the end of those who do not obey the gospel of God? Now

"If the righteous one is scarcely saved,
Where will the ungodly and the sinner
    appear?"
Therefore let those who suffer according to the
    will of God commit their souls to Him in
    doing good, as to a faithful Creator.

—1 PETER 4:12–19

"Blessed are you when they revile and persecute you, and say all kinds of evil against you falsely for My sake. Rejoice and be exceedingly glad, for great is your reward in heaven, for so they persecuted the prophets who were before you."

—MATTHEW 5:11–12

I'll Always Feel Unsettled about Life

To everything there is a season,
A time for every purpose under heaven:
A time to be born,
And a time to die;
A time to plant,
And a time to pluck what is planted;
A time to kill,
And a time to heal;
A time to break down,
And a time to build up;
A time to weep,
And a time to laugh;
A time to mourn,
And a time to dance;
A time to cast away stones,
And a time to gather stones;
A time to embrace,
And a time to refrain from embracing;
A time to gain,
And a time to lose;
A time to keep,
And a time to throw away;
A time to tear,
And a time to sew;
A time to keep silence,
And a time to speak;
A time to love,
And a time to hate;
A time of war,

And a time of peace. . . .
He has made everything beautiful in its time.
Also He has put eternity in their hearts,
    except that no one can find out the work
    that God does from beginning to end.

—ECCLESIASTES 3:1–8, 11

I Wish I'd Never Been Born

And Job spoke, and said:
"May the day perish on which I was born,
And the night in which it was said,
'A male child is conceived.'
May that day be darkness;
May God above not seek it,
Nor the light shine upon it.
May darkness and the shadow of death claim
    it;
May a cloud settle on it;
May the blackness of the day terrify it.
As for that night, may darkness seize it;
May it not be included among the days of the
    year,
May it not come into the number of the
    months.
Oh, may that night be barren!
May no joyful shout come into it!
May those curse it who curse the day,
Those who are ready to arouse Leviathan.
May the stars of its morning be dark;
May it look for light, but have none,

And not see the dawning of the day;
Because it did not shut up the doors of my
  mother's womb,
Nor hide sorrow from my eyes.

"Why did I not die at birth?
Why did I not perish when I came from the
  womb?
Why did the knees receive me?
Or why the breasts, that I should nurse?
For now I would have lain still and been quiet
  I would have been asleep;
Then I would have been at rest. . . ."

—JOB 3:2–13

. . . But:

Then God said, "Let Us make man in Our image, according to Our likeness; let them have dominion over the fish of the sea, over the birds of the air, and over the cattle, over all the earth and over every creeping thing that creeps on the earth." So God created man in His own image; in the image of God He created him; male and female He created them. Then God blessed them, and God said to them, "Be fruitful and multiply; fill the earth and subdue it; have dominion over the fish of the sea, over the birds of the air, and over every living thing that moves on the earth." And God said, "See, I have given you every herb that yields seed which is on the face of all the earth, and every tree whose fruit yields seed; to you it shall be for food. Also, to every beast of the earth, to every bird of the air, and to everything that creeps on the earth, in which there is life, I have given every green herb for food"; and it was so. Then God saw everything that He had made, and indeed it was very good.

—GENESIS 1:26–31a

I will praise You, for I am fearfully and
wonderfully made;
Marvelous are Your works,
And that my soul knows very well.
My frame was not hidden from You,
When I was made in secret,
And skillfully wrought in the lowest parts of
the earth.
Your eyes saw my substance, being yet
unformed.
And in Your book they all were written,
The days fashioned for me,
When as yet there were none of them.

—PSALM 139:14–16

New Experiences

Consider the many activities and relationships attached to a chemical dependency: where we go, what we do, whom we are with. In addition to the addictive agent itself is the routine attached to using it, and the people involved in supporting the life-style. Therefore, to give up an addiction means more than "never touching the stuff" again. It means starting into a whole new way of life, cutting ties with the past activities and the people associated with them.

How can we make such a radical break? By accentuating the new, positive activities and relationships that are waiting to replace the old ones. Be assured: The void must be filled with new, healthy experiences, or it will simply be filled again with other addictions. In the Scriptures, Jesus put it this way: "When an unclean spirit goes out of a man, he goes through dry places, seeking rest, and finds none. Then he says, 'I will return to my house from which I came.' And when he comes, he finds it empty, swept, and put in order. Then he goes and takes with him seven other spirits more wicked than himself, and they enter and dwell there; and the last state of that man is worse than the first" (Matthew 12:43–45a).

―――――――

Giving Up the Old Ways

Therefore, if anyone is in Christ, he is a new creation; old things have passed away; behold, all things have become new.

—2 CORINTHIANS 5:17

Therefore put to death your members which are on the earth: fornication, uncleanness, passion, evil desire, and covetousness, which is idolatry. Because of these things the wrath of God is coming upon the sons of disobedience, in which you also once walked when you lived in them. But now you must also put off all these: anger, wrath, malice, blasphemy, filthy language out of your mouth.

—COLOSSIANS 3:5–8

Therefore we also, since we are surrounded by so great a cloud of witnesses, let us lay aside every weight, and the sin which so easily ensnares us, and let us run with endurance the race that is set before us, looking unto Jesus, the author and finisher of our faith, who for the joy that was set before Him endured the cross, despising the shame, and has sat down at the right hand of the throne of God.

—HEBREWS 12:1-2

Therefore gird up the loins of your mind, be sober, and rest your hope fully upon the grace that is to be brought to you at the revelation of Jesus Christ; as obedient children, not conforming yourselves to the former lusts, as in your ignorance; but as He who called you is holy, you also be holy in all your conduct, because it is written, "Be holy, for I am holy."

—1 PETER 1:13-16

What shall we say then? Shall we continue in sin that grace may abound? Certainly not! How shall we who died to sin live any longer in it? Or do you not know that as many of us as were baptized into Christ Jesus were baptized into His death? Therefore we were buried with Him through baptism into death, that just as Christ was raised from the dead by the glory of the Father, even so we also should walk in newness of life. . . . Likewise you also, reckon yourselves to be dead indeed to sin, but alive to God in Christ Jesus our Lord. Therefore do not let sin reign in your mortal body, that you should obey it in its lusts.

—ROMANS 6:1-4, 11-12

Walking In a New Way

Walk in the Spirit, and you shall not fulfill the lust of the flesh. For the flesh lusts against the Spirit, and the Spirit against the flesh; and these are contrary to one another, so that you do not do the things that you wish.

—GALATIANS 5:16b–17

This I say, therefore, and testify in the Lord, that you should no longer walk as the rest of the Gentiles walk, in the futility of their mind, having their understanding darkened, being alienated from the life of God, because of the ignorance that is in them, because of the hardness of their heart; who, being past feeling, have given themselves over to licentiousness, to work all uncleanness with greediness. But you have not so learned Christ, if indeed you have heard Him and have been taught by Him, as the truth is in Jesus: that you put off, concerning your former conduct, the old man which grows corrupt according to the deceitful lusts, and be renewed in the spirit of your mind.

—EPHESIANS 4:17–23

For you were once darkness, but now you are light in the Lord. Walk as children of light (for the fruit of the Spirit is in all goodness, righteousness, and truth), proving what is acceptable to the Lord.

—EPHESIANS 5:8–10

And do this, knowing the time, that now it is high time to awake out of sleep; for now our salvation is nearer than when we first believed. The night is far spent, the day is at hand. Therefore let us cast off the works of darkness, and let us put on the armor of light. Let us walk properly, as in the day, not in revelry and drunkenness, not in licentiousness and lewdness, not in strife and envy. But put on the Lord Jesus Christ, and make no provision for the flesh, to fulfill its lusts.

—ROMANS 13:11–14

For we have spent enough of our past lifetime in doing the will of the Gentiles—when we walked in lewdness, lusts, drunkenness, revelries, drinking parties, and abominable idolatries.

—1 PETER 4:3

Being Willing to Set Boundaries

■ *Setting Boundaries in Relationships*

Paul confronts a friend . . .

But when Peter had come to Antioch, I withstood him to his face, because he was to be blamed; for before certain men came from James, he would eat with the Gentiles; but when they came, he withdrew and separated himself, fearing those who were of the circumcision. And the rest of the Jews also played the hypocrite with him, so that even Barnabas was carried away with their hypocrisy. But when I saw that they were not straightforward about the truth of the gospel, I said to Peter before them all, "If you, being a Jew, live in the manner of Gentiles and not as the Jews, why do you compel Gentiles to live as Jews? We who are Jews by nature, and not sinners of the Gentiles, knowing that a man is not justified by the works of the law but by faith in Jesus Christ, even we have believed in Christ Jesus, that we might be justified by faith in Christ and not by the works of the law; for by the works of the law no flesh shall be justified. But if, while we seek to be justified by Christ, we ourselves also are found sinners, is Christ therefore a minister of sin? Certainly not! For if I build again those things which I destroyed, I make myself a transgressor. For I through the law died to the law that I might live to God. I have been crucified with Christ; it is no longer I who live, but Christ lives in me; and the life which I now live in the flesh I live by faith in the Son of God, who loved me and gave Himself for me. I do not set aside the grace of God; for if righteousness comes through the law, then Christ died in vain."

—GALATIANS 2:11-21

. . . And we must confront one another, too.

"Moreover if your brother sins against you, go and tell him his fault between you and him alone.

If he hears you, you have gained your brother. But if he will not hear, take with you one or two more, that 'by the mouth of two or three witnesses every word may be established.' And if he refuses to hear them, tell it to the church. But if he refuses even to hear the church, let him be to you like a heathen and a tax collector."

—MATTHEW 18:15–17

Therefore, putting away lying, each one speak truth with his neighbor, for we are members of one another.

—EPHESIANS 4:25

■ Setting Boundaries in Sexual Matters

"I have made a covenant with my eyes;
Why then should I look upon a young
   woman? . . .

"If my heart has been enticed by a woman,
Or if I have lurked at my neighbor's door,
Then let my wife grind for another,
And let others bow down over her.
For that would be wickedness;
Yes, it would be iniquity worthy of judgment.
For that would be a fire that consumes to
   destruction,
And would root out all my increase."

—JOB 31:1, 9–12

For at the window of my house I looked
   through my lattice,

And saw among the simple, I perceived
    among the youths,
A young man devoid of understanding,
Passing along the street near her corner;
And he took the path to her house
In the twilight, in the evening,
In the black and dark night.
And there a woman met him,
With the attire of a harlot, and a crafty heart.
She was loud and rebellious,
Her feet would not stay at home.
At times she was outside, at times in the open
    square,
Lurking at every corner.
So she caught him and kissed him;
With an impudent face she said to him:
"I have peace offerings with me;
Today I have paid my vows.
So I came out to meet you,
Diligently to seek your face,
And I have found you.
I have spread my bed with tapestry,
Colored coverings of Egyptian linen.
I have perfumed my bed
With myrrh, aloes, and cinnamon.
Come, let us take our fill of love until
    morning;
Let us delight ourselves with love.
For my husband is not at home;
He has gone on a long journey;
He has taken a bag of money with him,

And will come home on the appointed day."
With her enticing speech she caused him to
    yield,
With her flattering lips she seduced him.
Immediately he went after her, as an ox goes
    to the slaughter,
Or as a fool to the correction of the stocks.

                    —PROVERBS 7:6–22

■ Setting Boundaries in Financial Matters

Now Jesus sat opposite the treasury and saw how the people put money into the treasury. And many who were rich put in much. Then one poor widow came and threw in two mites, which make a quadrans. So He called His disciples to Him and said to them, "Assuredly, I say to you that this poor widow has put in more than all those who have given to the treasury; for they all put in out of their abundance, but she out of her poverty put in all that she had, her whole livelihood."

                    —MARK 12:41–44

"Do not fear, little flock, for it is your Father's good pleasure to give you the kingdom. Sell what you have and give alms; provide yourselves money bags which do not grow old, a treasure in the heavens that does not fail, where no thief approaches nor moth destroys. For where your treasure is, there your heart will be also."

                    —LUKE 12:32–34

But godliness with contentment is great gain. For we brought nothing into this world, and it is certain we can carry nothing out. And having food and clothing, with these we shall be content. But those who desire to be rich fall into temptation and a snare, and into many foolish and harmful lusts which drown men in destruction and perdition. For the love of money is a root of all kinds of evil, for which some have strayed from the faith in their greediness, and pierced themselves through with many sorrows. But you, O man of God, flee these things and pursue righteousness, godliness, faith, love, patience, gentleness.

—1 TIMOTHY 6:6–11

■ Setting Boundaries with Food and Drink

For none of us lives to himself, and no one dies to himself. For if we live, we live to the Lord; and if we die, we die to the Lord. Therefore, whether we live or die, we are the Lord's. For to this end Christ died and rose and lived again, that He might be Lord of both the dead and the living. . . . So then each of us shall give account of himself to God. Therefore let us not judge one another anymore, but rather resolve this, not to put a stumbling block or a cause to fall in our brother's way. I know and am convinced by the Lord Jesus that there is nothing unclean of itself; but to him who considers anything to be unclean, to him it is unclean. . . . for the kingdom of God is not food and drink, but righteousness and peace and joy in the Holy Spirit. . . . It is good neither to eat meat nor drink wine nor do anything by which your brother stumbles or is offended or is made weak. Do you have faith? Have it to yourself before God. Happy is he who does not condemn himself in what he approves.

—ROMANS 14:7–9, 12–14, 17, 21–22

Being Willing to Ask for Help

I will lift up my eyes to the hills—
From whence comes my help?
My help comes from the LORD,
Who made heaven and earth.
He will not allow your foot to be moved;
He who keeps you will not slumber.
Behold, He who keeps Israel
Shall neither slumber nor sleep.
The LORD is your keeper;
The LORD is your shade at your right hand.
The sun shall not strike you by day,
Nor the moon by night.
The LORD shall preserve you from all evil;
He shall preserve your soul.
The LORD shall preserve your going out and
    your coming in
From this time forth, and even forevermore.

—PSALM 121:1–8

O God, do not be far from me;
O my God, make haste to help me!

Let them be confounded and consumed
Who are adversaries of my life;
Let them be covered with reproach and
    dishonor
Who seek my hurt.
But I will hope continually,
And will praise You yet more and more.
My mouth shall tell of Your righteousness
And Your salvation all the day, For I do not
    know their limits.
I will go in the strength of the Lord GOD;
I will make mention of Your righteousness, of
    Yours only.
O God, You have taught me from my youth;
And to this day I declare Your wondrous
    works.
Now also when I am old and gray-headed, O
    God, do not forsake me,
Until I declare Your strength to this
    generation,
Your power to everyone who is to come.
Also Your righteousness, O God, is very high,
You who have done great things; O God, who
    is like You?

—PSALM 71:12–19

And there is no creature hidden from His sight,
but all things are naked and open to the eyes of
Him to whom we must give account. Seeing then
that we have a great High Priest who has passed
through the heavens, Jesus the Son of God, let us
hold fast our confession. For we do not have a

High Priest who cannot sympathize with our weaknesses, but was in all points tempted as we are, yet without sin. Let us therefore come boldly to the throne of grace, that we may obtain mercy and find grace to help in time of need.

—HEBREWS 4:13–16

Reparenting

Those of us raised in dysfunctional families know what it means to be orphaned. Even if both parents were physically present in the home, their withdrawal of emotional support often felt like sheer abandonment. Now we have this gaping nurture-deficit crying out deep within us. How will we fill it? To whom can we turn for the lost care and comfort?

Look around you. What one person might be waiting for you, with some nurture to give? It will not be easy to find such a person, since almost everyone has experienced some form of deprivation in their families of origin. Yet there are those who have worked through the pain. They have come to a point of being able to give rather than constantly take. May you find that special person to be your new friend, someone who can help you by filling a parenting role on a healthy, informal basis.

The Scriptures in this chapter suggest another resource, too: God as Heavenly Parent.

Have you sensed that God has all the qualities you so longed for in your own earthly parents: unconditional love, care, closeness? The Bible offers so much hope that those needs can be met through God and His people. Seek and you will find.

Being Reparented by God, Our Heavenly Father

> But now, O LORD, You are our Father;
> We are the clay, and You our potter;
> And all we are the work of Your hand.
> —ISAIAH 64:8

> A father of the fatherless, a defender of widows,
> Is God in His holy habitation.
> —PSALM 68:5

"In My Father's house are many mansions; if it were not so, I would have told you. I go to prepare a place for you. And if I go and prepare a place for you, I will come again and receive you to Myself; that where I am, there you may be also. And where I go you know, and the way you know." Thomas said to Him, "Lord, we do not know where You are going, and how can we know the way?" Jesus said to him, "I am the way, the truth, and the life. No one comes to the Father except through Me. If you had known Me, you would have known My Father also; and from now on you know Him and have seen Him." Philip said to Him, "Lord, show us the Father, and it is sufficient for us." Jesus said to him, "Have I been with you so long, and yet you have not known Me, Philip? He who has seen Me has seen the Father. . . ."

—JOHN 14:2–9a

"These things I have spoken to you while being present with you. But the Helper, the Holy Spirit, whom the Father will send in My name, He will teach you all things, and bring to your remembrance all things that I said to you. Peace I leave with you, My peace I give to you; not as the world gives do I give to you. Let not your heart be troubled, neither let it be afraid."

—JOHN 14:25–27

Now may our Lord Jesus Christ Himself, and our God and Father, who has loved us and given us everlasting consolation and good hope by grace, comfort your hearts and establish you in every good word and work.

—2 THESSALONIANS 2:16–17

■ *He Loves Us Unconditionally*

He who does not love does not know God, for God is love. In this the love of God was manifested toward us, that God has sent His only begotten Son into the world, that we might live through Him. In this is love, not that we loved God, but that He loved us and sent His Son to be the propitiation for our sins. Beloved, if God so loved us, we also ought to love one another. No one has seen God at any time. If we love one another, God abides in us, and His love has been perfected in us. By this we know that we abide in Him, and He in us, because He has given us of His Spirit. And we have seen and testify that the Father has sent the Son as Savior of the world. Whoever confesses that Jesus is the Son of God, God abides in him, and he in God. And we have known and believed the love that God has for us. God is love, and he who abides in love abides in God, and God in him. Love has been perfected among us in this: that we may have boldness in the day of judgment; because as He is, so are we in this world. There is no fear in love; but perfect love casts out fear, because fear involves torment. But he who fears has not been made perfect in love. We love Him because He first loved us.

—1 JOHN 4:8–19

■ He Accepts Us Apart from Our Own Merit

But God, who is rich in mercy, because of His great love with which He loved us, even when we were dead in trespasses, made us alive together with Christ (by grace you have been saved), and raised us up together, and made us sit together in the heavenly places in Christ Jesus, that in the ages to come He might show the exceeding riches of His grace in His kindness toward us in Christ Jesus. For by grace you have been saved through faith, and that not of yourselves; it is the gift of God, not of works, lest anyone should boast.

—EPHESIANS 2:4-9

For we ourselves were also once foolish, disobedient, deceived, serving various lusts and pleasures, living in malice and envy, hateful and hating one another. But when the kindness and the love of God our Savior toward man appeared, not by works of righteousness which we have done, but according to His mercy He saved us, through the washing of regeneration and renewing of the Holy Spirit, whom He poured out on us abundantly through Jesus Christ our Savior, that having been justified by His grace we should become heirs according to the hope of eternal life.

—TITUS 3:3-7

■ He Adopts Us as His Own Children

For as many as are led by the Spirit of God, these are sons of God. For you did not receive the spirit of bondage again to fear, but you received the Spirit of adoption by whom we cry out, "Abba, Father." The Spirit Himself bears witness with our spirit that we are children of God, and if children, then heirs—heirs of God and joint heirs with Christ, if indeed we suffer with Him, that we may also be glorified together. For I consider that the sufferings of this present time are not worthy to be compared with the glory which shall be revealed in us. For the earnest expectation of the creation eagerly waits for the revealing of the sons of God. For the creation was subjected to futility, not willingly, but because of Him who subjected it in hope; because the creation itself also will be delivered from the bondage of corruption into the glorious liberty of the children of God. For we know that the whole creation groans and labors with birth pangs together until now.

—ROMANS 8:14–22

Even so we, when we were children, were in bondage under the elements of the world. But when the fullness of the time had come, God sent forth His Son, born of a woman, born under the law, to redeem those who were under the law, that we might receive the adoption as sons. And because you are sons, God has sent forth the Spirit of His Son into your hearts, crying out, "Abba, Father!" Therefore you are no longer a slave but a son, and if a son, then an heir of God through Christ.

—GALATIANS 4:3–7

■ He Disciplines Us In Love

"My son, do not despise the chastening of the
  LORD,
Nor be discouraged when you are rebuked by
  Him;

For whom the LORD loves He chastens,
And scourges every son whom He receives."

If you endure chastening, God deals with you as with sons; for what son is there whom a father does not chasten? But if you are without chastening, of which all have become partakers, then you are illegitimate and not sons. Furthermore, we have had human fathers who corrected us, and we paid them respect. Shall we not much more readily be in subjection to the Father of spirits and live? For they indeed for a few days chastened us as seemed best to them, but He for our profit, that we may be partakers of His holiness. Now no chastening seems to be joyful for the present, but grievous; nevertheless, afterward it yields the peaceable fruit of righteousness to those who have been trained by it.

—HEBREWS 12:5b–11

■ *He Guides Us*

So God led the people around by way of the wilderness of the Red Sea. And the children of Israel went up in orderly ranks out of the land of Egypt. . . . And the LORD went before them by day in a pillar of cloud to lead the way, and by night in a pillar of fire to give them light, so as to go by day and night. He did not take away the pillar of cloud by day or the pillar of fire by night from before the people.

—EXODUS 13:18, 21–22

"Comfort, yes, comfort My people!"
Says your God. . . .
He will feed His flock like a shepherd;
He will gather the lambs with His arm,
And carry them in His bosom,
And gently lead those who are with
    young. . . .
Lift up your eyes on high,
And see who has created these things,
Who brings out their host by number;
He calls them all by name,
By the greatness of His might
And the strength of His power;
Not one is missing. . . .
Have you not known?
Have you not heard?
The everlasting God, the LORD,
The Creator of the ends of the earth,
Neither faints nor is weary.
There is no searching of His understanding.
He gives power to the weak,
And to those who have no might He increases
    strength.
Even the youths shall faint and be weary,
And the young men shall utterly fall,
But those who wait on the LORD
Shall renew their strength;
They shall mount up with wings like eagles,
They shall run and not be weary,
They shall walk and not faint.

—ISAIAH 40:1, 11, 26, 28–31

■ *He Stays Close, Calming our Fears*

"Fear not, for I have redeemed you;
I have called you by your name;
You are Mine.
When you pass through the waters, I will be
    with you;
And through the rivers, they shall not
    overflow you.
When you walk through the fire, you shall not
    be burned,
Nor shall the flame scorch you.
For I am the LORD your God,
The Holy One of Israel, your Savior;
I gave Egypt for your ransom,
Ethiopia and Seba in your place.
Since you were precious in My sight,
You have been honored,
And I have loved you;
Therefore I will give men for you,
And people for your life.
Fear not, for I am with you;
I will bring your descendants from the
    east,
And gather you from the west;
I will say to the north, 'Give them up!'
And to the south, 'Do not keep them back!'
Bring My sons from afar,
And My daughters from the ends of the
    earth—
Everyone who is called by My name,

Whom I have created for My glory;
I have formed him, yes, I have made him."

—ISAIAH 43:1b–7

Getting Support from God's People

Be kindly affectionate to one another with brotherly love, in honor giving preference to one another.

—ROMANS 12:10

[And] comfort each other and edify one another, just as you also are doing. . . . Now we exhort you, brethren, warn those who are unruly, comfort the fainthearted, uphold the weak, be patient with all.

—1 THESSALONIANS 5:11, 14

Not forsaking the assembling of ourselves together, as is the manner of some, but exhorting one another, and so much the more as you see the Day approaching.

—HEBREWS 10:25

For as the body is one and has many members, but all the members of that one body, being many, are one body, so also is Christ. For by one Spirit we were all baptized into one body—whether Jews or Greeks, whether slaves or free—and have all been made to drink into one Spirit. For in fact the body is not one member but many. If the foot should say, "Because I am not a hand, I am not of the body," is it therefore not of the body? And if the ear should say, "Because I am not an eye, I am not of the body," is it therefore not of the body? If the whole body were an eye, where would be the hearing? If the whole were hearing, where would be the smelling? But now God has set the members, each one of them, in the body just as He pleased. And if they were all one member, where would the body be? But now indeed there are many members, yet one body. And the eye cannot say to the hand, "I have no need of you"; nor again the head to the feet, "I have no need of you." No, much rather, those members of the body which seem to be weaker are necessary. And those members of the body which we think to be less honorable, on these we bestow greater honor; and our unpresentable parts have greater modesty, but our presentable parts have no need. But God composed the body, having given greater honor to that part which lacks it, that there should be no schism in the body, but that the members should have the same care for one another. And if one member suffers, all the members suffer with it; or if one member is honored, all the members rejoice with it.

—1 CORINTHIANS 12:12–26

CHAPTER

9

Accountability

Being accountable takes some courage. Who wouldn't rather take the phone off the hook than "face the music" of creditors, teachers, bosses, or others we've let down? But the Scriptures call us to replace the receiver and let the calls come in. We must listen to hear and face our responsibilities, while setting reasonable boundaries for ourselves.

Yes, it may take courage, but the good news is that accountability feeds on itself. Each small act of responsible behavior makes it easier to follow through on the next project. And our reputation for dependability grows with each success.

Accountability to the Victims of My Compulsions

■ *David Follows His Craving . . .*

So David sent and inquired about the woman. And someone said, "Is this not Bathsheba, the daughter of Eliam, the wife of Uriah the Hittite? . . ." Then David sent to Joab, saying, "Send me Uriah the Hittite." And Joab sent Uriah to David. . . . In the morning it was so that David wrote a letter to Joab and sent it by the hand of Uriah. And he wrote in the letter, saying, "Set Uriah in the forefront of the hottest battle, and retreat from him, that he may be struck down and die." So it happened, while Joab besieged the city, that he assigned Uriah to a place where he knew there were valiant men. Then the men of the city came out and fought with Joab. And some of the people of the servants of David fell; and Uriah the Hittite died also.

—2 SAMUEL 11:3, 6, 14–17

■ . . . *Which Results in Murder*

When the wife of Uriah heard that Uriah her husband was dead, she mourned for her husband.

—2 SAMUEL 11:26

[And Nathan said to David]: "Why have you despised the commandment of the LORD, to do evil in His sight? You have killed Uriah the Hittite with the sword; you have taken his wife to be your wife, and have killed him with the sword of the people of Ammon."

—2 SAMUEL 12:9

Therefore you are inexcusable, O man, whoever you are who judge, for in whatever you judge an-

other you condemn yourself; for you who judge
practice the same things.

—ROMANS 2:1

Accountability with Addictive Agents

■ *Because of Drunkenness, Noah Fails with His Son . . .*

Now the sons of Noah who went out of the ark
were Shem, Ham, and Japheth. And Ham was the
father of Canaan. These three were the sons of
Noah, and from these the whole earth was popu-
lated. And Noah began to be a farmer, and he
planted a vineyard. Then he drank of the wine and
was drunk, and became uncovered in his tent.
And Ham, the father of Canaan, saw the nakedness of his father, and told his two brothers outside. But Shem and Japheth took a garment, laid it
on both their shoulders, and went backward and
covered the nakedness of their father. Their faces
were turned away, and they did not see their
father's nakedness. So Noah awoke from his
wine, and knew what his younger son had done to
him. Then he said:

> "Cursed be Canaan;
> A servant of servants
> He shall be to his brethren."

—GENESIS 9:18–25

■ . . . *And Lot Failed with His Daughters*

Then Lot went up out of Zoar and dwelt in the mountains, and his two daughters were with him; for he was afraid to dwell in Zoar. And he and his two daughters dwelt in a cave. Now the firstborn said to the younger, "Our father is old, and there is no man on the earth to come in to us as is the custom of all the earth. Come, let us make our father drink wine, and we will lie with him, that we may preserve the lineage of our father." So they made their father drink wine that night. And the firstborn went in and lay with her father, and he did not know when she lay down or when she arose. It happened on the next day that the firstborn said to the younger, "Indeed I lay with my father last night; let us make him drink wine tonight also, and you go in and lie with him, that we may preserve the lineage of our father." Then they made their father drink wine that night also. And the younger arose and lay with him, and he did not know when she lay down or when she arose. Thus both the daughters of Lot were with child by their father.

—GENESIS 19:30–36

Accountability to the New Commandment: Love

"A new commandment I give to you, that you love one another; as I have loved you, that you also

love one another. By this all will know that you are
My disciples, if you have love for one another."
—JOHN 13:34–35

Though I speak with the tongues of men and of
angels, but have not love, I have become as sounding brass or a clanging cymbal. And though I have
the gift of prophecy, and understand all mysteries
and all knowledge, and though I have all faith, so
that I could remove mountains, but have not love,
I am nothing. And though I bestow all my goods
to feed the poor, and though I give my body to be
burned, but have not love, it profits me nothing.
Love suffers long and is kind; love does not envy;
love does not parade itself, is not puffed up; does
not behave rudely, does not seek its own, is not
provoked, thinks no evil; does not rejoice in iniquity, but rejoices in the truth; bears all things, believes all things, hopes all things, endures all
things. Love never fails. But whether there are
prophecies, they will fail; whether there are
tongues, they will cease; whether there is knowledge, it will vanish away. For we know in part and
we prophesy in part. But when that which is perfect has come, then that which is in part will be
done away. When I was a child, I spoke as a child,
I understood as a child, I thought as a child; but
when I became a man, I put away childish things.
For now we see in a mirror, dimly, but then face to
face. Now I know in part, but then I shall know
just as I also am known. And now abide faith,

hope, love, these three; but the greatest of these is love.

—1 CORINTHIANS 13:1–13

■ *Love Your Brother*

Behold, how good and how pleasant it is
For brethren to dwell together in unity!
It is like the precious oil upon the head,
Running down on the beard,
The beard of Aaron,
Running down on the edge of his garments.
It is like the dew of Hermon,
Descending upon the mountains of Zion;
For there the LORD commanded the blessing—
Life forevermore.

—PSALM 133:1–3

For none of us lives to himself, and no one dies to himself. For if we live, we live to the Lord; and if we die, we die to the Lord. Therefore, whether we live or die, we are the Lord's. For to this end Christ died and rose and lived again, that He might be Lord of both the dead and the living. But why do you judge your brother? Or why do you show contempt for your brother? For we shall all stand before the judgment seat of Christ.

—ROMANS 14:7–10

If someone says, "I love God," and hates his brother, he is a liar; for he who does not love his brother whom he has seen, how can he love God

whom he has not seen? And this commandment
we have from Him: that he who loves God must
love his brother also.

—1 JOHN 4:20–21

Finally, all of you be of one mind, having compassion for one another; love as brothers, be ten-
derhearted, be courteous; not returning evil for
evil or reviling for reviling, but on the contrary
blessing, knowing that you were called to this,
that you may inherit a blessing. For

"He who would love life
And see good days,
Let him refrain his tongue from evil,
And his lips from speaking guile;
Let him turn away from evil and do good;
Let him seek peace and pursue it.
For the eyes of the LORD are on the righteous,
And His ears are open to their prayers;
But the face of the LORD is against those who
    do evil."

—1 PETER 3:8–12

■ Love Your Enemy

"You have heard that it was said, 'You shall love
your neighbor and hate your enemy.' But I say to
you, love your enemies, bless those who curse
you, do good to those who hate you, and pray for
those who spitefully use you and persecute you,
that you may be sons of your Father in heaven; for

He makes His sun rise on the evil and on the good, and sends rain on the just and on the unjust. For if you love those who love you, what reward have you? Do not even the tax collectors do the same? And if you greet your brethren only, what do you do more than others? Do not even the tax collectors do so?"

—MATTHEW 5:43–47

■ *Love Those in Need*

And behold, a certain lawyer stood up and tested Him, saying, "Teacher, what shall I do to inherit eternal life?" He said to him, "What is written in the law? What is your reading of it?" So he answered and said, "'You shall love the LORD your God with all your heart, with all your soul, with all your strength, and with all your mind,' and 'your neighbor as yourself.'" And He said to him, "You have answered rightly; do this and you will live." But he, wanting to justify himself, said to Jesus, "And who is my neighbor?" Then Jesus answered and said: "A certain man went down from Jerusalem to Jericho, and fell among thieves, who stripped him of his clothing, wounded him, and departed, leaving him half dead. Now by chance a certain priest came down that road. And when he saw him, he passed by on the other side. Likewise a Levite, when he arrived at the place, came and looked, and passed by on the other side. But a certain Samaritan, as he journeyed, came where he was. And when he saw him, he had compassion on him, and went to him and bandaged his wounds, pouring on oil and wine; and he set him on his own animal, brought him to an inn, and took care of him. On the next day, when he departed, he took out two denarii, gave them to the innkeeper, and said to him, 'Take care of him; and whatever more you spend, when I come again, I will repay you.' So which of these three do you think was neighbor to him who fell among the thieves?" And he said, "He who showed mercy on him." Then Jesus said to him, "Go and do likewise."

—LUKE 10:25–37

Accountability in Choice of Friends

Blessed is the man
Who walks not in the counsel of the ungodly,
Nor stands in the path of sinners,
Nor sits in the seat of the scornful;
But his delight is in the law of the LORD,
And in His law he meditates day and night.
He shall be like a tree
Planted by the rivers of water,
That brings forth its fruit in its season,
Whose leaf also shall not wither;
And whatever he does shall prosper.
The ungodly are not so,
But are like the chaff which the wind drives
    away.

Therefore the ungodly shall not stand in the
    judgment,
Nor sinners in the congregation of the
    righteous.
For the LORD knows the way of the righteous,
But the way of the ungodly shall perish.
                                    —PSALM 1:1–6

Accountability to Authority

Let every soul be subject to the governing authorities. For there is no authority except from
God, and the authorities that exist are appointed
by God. Therefore whoever resists the authority
resists the ordinance of God, and those who resist
will bring judgment on themselves. For rulers are
not a terror to good works, but to evil. Do you
want to be unafraid of the authority? Do what is
good, and you will have praise from the same. For
he is God's minister to you for good. But if you do
evil, be afraid; for he does not bear the sword in
vain; for he is God's minister, an avenger to exe-
cute wrath on him who practices evil. Therefore
you must be subject, not only because of wrath
but also for conscience' sake. For because of this
you also pay taxes, for they are God's ministers
attending continually to this very thing. Render
therefore to all their due: taxes to whom taxes are
due, customs to whom customs, fear to whom
fear, honor to whom honor. Owe no one anything

except to love one another, for he who loves another has fulfilled the law.

—ROMANS 13:1–8

Let us walk properly, as in the day, not in revelry and drunkenness, not in licentiousness and lewdness, not in strife and envy. But put on the Lord Jesus Christ, and make no provision for the flesh, to fulfill its lusts.

—ROMANS 13:13–14

But Jesus called them to Himself and said, "You know that the rulers of the Gentiles lord it over them, and those who are great exercise authority over them. Yet it shall not be so among you; but whoever desires to become great among you, let him be your servant. And whoever desires to be first among you, let him be your slave—just as the Son of Man did not come to be served, but to serve, and to give His life a ransom for many."

—MATTHEW 20:25–28

Accountability in Marriage and Sexuality

It is good for a man not to touch a woman. Nevertheless, because of sexual immorality, let each man have his own wife, and let each woman have her own husband. Let the husband render to his wife the affection due her, and likewise also the wife to her husband. The wife does not have authority over her own body, but the husband does. And likewise the husband does not have authority over his own body, but the wife does. Do not deprive one another except with consent for a time, that you may give yourselves to fasting and prayer; and come together again so that Satan does not tempt you because of your lack of self-control. But I say this as a concession, not as a commandment. For I wish that all men were even as I myself. But each one has his own gift from God, one in this manner and another in that. But I say to the unmarried and to the widows: It is good for them if they remain even as I am; but if they cannot exercise self-control, let them marry. For it is better to marry than to burn with passion. Now to the married I command, yet not I but the Lord: A wife is not to depart from her husband. But even if she does depart, let her remain unmarried or be reconciled to her husband. And a husband is not to divorce his wife. But to the rest I, not the Lord, say: If any brother has a wife who does not believe, and she is willing to live with him, let him not divorce her. And a woman who has a husband who does not believe, if he is willing to live with her, let her not divorce him. For the unbelieving husband is sanctified by the wife, and the unbelieving wife is sanctified by the husband; otherwise your children would be unclean, but now they are holy. But if the unbeliever departs, let him depart; a brother or a sister is not under bondage in such cases. But God has called us to peace. For how do you know, O wife, whether you will save your husband? Or how do you know, O husband, whether you will save your wife?

—1 CORINTHIANS 7:1b–16

For this is the will of God, your sanctification: that you should abstain from sexual immorality; that each of you should know how to possess his own vessel in sanctification and honor, not in passion of lust, like the Gentiles who do not know God; that no one should take advantage of and defraud his brother in this matter, because the Lord is the avenger of all such, as we also forewarned you and testified. For God did not call us to uncleanness, but in holiness. Therefore he who rejects this does not reject man, but God, who has also given us His Holy Spirit.

—1 THESSALONIANS 4:3–8

But fornication and all uncleanness or covetousness, let it not even be named among you, as is fitting for saints; neither filthiness, nor foolish talking, nor coarse jesting, which are not fitting, but rather giving of thanks. For this you know, that no fornicator, unclean person, nor covetous man, who is an idolater, has any inheritance in the kingdom of Christ and God. Let no one deceive you with empty words, for because of these things the wrath of God comes upon the sons of disobedience. Therefore do not be partakers with them. . . . And do not be drunk with wine, in which is dissipation; but be filled with the Spirit.

—EPHESIANS 5:3–7, 18

Accountability in Church Leadership

This is a faithful saying: If a man desires the position of a bishop, he desires a good work. A bishop then must be blameless, the husband of one wife, temperate, sober-minded, of good behavior, hospitable, able to teach; not given to wine, not violent, not greedy for money, but gentle, not quarrelsome, not covetous; one who rules his own house well, having his children in submission with all reverence (for if a man does not know how to rule his own house, how will he take care of the church of God?); not a novice, lest being puffed up with pride he fall into the same condemnation as the devil. Moreover he must have a good testimony among those who are outside, lest he fall into reproach and the snare of the devil. Likewise deacons must be reverent, not double-tongued, not given to much wine, not greedy for money, holding the mystery of the faith with a pure conscience.

—1 TIMOTHY 3:1–9

For a bishop must be blameless, as a steward of God, not self-willed, not quick-tempered, not given to wine, not violent, not greedy for money, but hospitable, a lover of what is good, sober-minded, just, holy, self-controlled, holding fast the faithful word as he has been taught, that he may be able, by sound doctrine, both to exhort and convict those who contradict.

—TITUS 1:7–9

But as for you, speak the things which are proper for sound doctrine: that the older men be sober, reverent, temperate, sound in faith, in love, in patience; the older women likewise, that they be reverent in behavior, not slanderers, not given to much wine, teachers of good things—that they admonish the young women to love their husbands, to love their children, to be discreet, chaste, homemakers, good, obedient to their own husbands, that the word of God may not be blasphemed. Likewise exhort the young men to be sober-minded, in all things showing yourself to be a pattern of good works; in doctrine showing integrity, reverence, incorruptibility, sound speech that cannot be condemned, that one who is an opponent may be ashamed, having nothing evil to say of you.

—TITUS 2:1–8

CHAPTER

10

Maintenance

New concept: Meet your needs! Another way to put it: Take care of yourself. People in recovery find that they get a lot of support when they take the time and energy to seek it out. But no matter how many "reparents" or close friends in recovery we gather around us, the fact remains: The only person who is going to make sure my needs are met is . . . me.

By meeting our needs for things like family life, leisure, worship, time alone, we protect ourselves against falling back into the old addictive patterns. Chemical dependencies fill—in a very imperfect way—the need for something else. Make sure you are getting enough of the something else instead!

The Bible offers fertile ground for exploring that something else: new, significant goals and life purposes, the benefits of prayer and Scripture reading, the wisdom of making life choices with eternal values in mind.

Maintaining My Devotional Life

■ *Regular Scripture Reading*

Blessed are the undefiled in the way,
Who walk in the law of the LORD!
Blessed are those who keep His testimonies,
Who seek Him with the whole heart!
They also do no iniquity;
They walk in His ways.
You have commanded us
To keep Your precepts diligently.
Oh, that my ways were directed
To keep Your statutes!
Then I would not be ashamed,
When I look into all Your commandments.
I will praise You with uprightness of heart,
When I learn Your righteous judgments.
I will keep Your statutes;
Oh, do not forsake me utterly!
How can a young man cleanse his way?
By taking heed according to Your word.
With my whole heart I have sought You;
Oh, let me not wander from Your
    commandments!
Your word I have hidden in my heart,
That I might not sin against You!
Blessed are You, O LORD!
Teach me Your statutes!
With my lips I have declared
All the judgments of Your mouth.
I have rejoiced in the way of Your testimonies,

As much as in all riches.
I will meditate on Your precepts,
And contemplate Your ways.
I will delight myself in Your statutes;
I will not forget Your word.

—PSALM 119:1-16

■ *Regular Prayer*

Pray without ceasing, in everything give
thanks; for this is the will of God in Christ Jesus
for you. Do not quench the Spirit. Do not despise
prophecies. Test all things; hold fast what is good.
Abstain from every form of evil.

—1 THESSALONIANS 5:17-22

Is anyone among you suffering? Let him pray. Is
anyone cheerful? Let him sing psalms. Is anyone
among you sick? Let him call for the elders of the
church, and let them pray over him, anointing
him with oil in the name of the Lord. And the
prayer of faith will save the sick, and the Lord will
raise him up. And if he has committed sins, he
will be forgiven. Confess your trespasses to one
another, and pray for one another, that you may be
healed. The effective, fervent prayer of a righteous
man avails much. Elijah was a man with a nature
like ours, and he prayed earnestly that it would
not rain; and it did not rain on the land for three
years and six months. And he prayed again, and

the heaven gave rain, and the earth produced its
fruit.

—JAMES 5:13–18

Avoiding Temptation with God's Provision

Keep me, O LORD, from the hands of the
  wicked;
Preserve me from violent men,
Who have purposed to make my steps
  stumble.

—PSALM 140:4

Now these things became our examples, to the
intent that we should not lust after evil things as
they also lusted. And do not become idolaters as
were some of them. As it is written, "The people
sat down to eat and drink, and rose up to play."
Nor let us commit sexual immorality, as some of
them did, and in one day twenty-three thousand
fell; nor let us tempt Christ, as some of them also
tempted, and were destroyed by serpents; nor
murmur, as some of them also murmured, and
were destroyed by the destroyer. Now all these
things happened to them as examples, and they
were written for our admonition, on whom the
ends of the ages have come. Therefore let him who
thinks he stands take heed lest he fall. No temptation has overtaken you except such as is common
to man; but God is faithful, who will not allow you

to be tempted beyond what you are able, but with the temptation will also make the way of escape, that you may be able to bear it.

—1 CORINTHIANS 10:6-13

But the Lord is faithful, who will establish you and guard you from the evil one. And we have confidence in the Lord concerning you, both that you do and will do the things we command you. Now may the Lord direct your hearts into the love of God and into the patience of Christ.

—2 THESSALONIANS 3:3

The LORD is merciful and gracious,
Slow to anger, and abounding in mercy.
He will not always strive with us,
Nor will He keep His anger forever.
He has not dealt with us according to our
    sins,
Nor punished us according to our iniquities.
For as the heavens are high above the earth,
So great is His mercy toward those who fear
    Him;
As far as the east is from the west,
So far has He removed our transgressions
    from us.
As a father pities his children,
So the LORD pities those who fear Him.
For He knows our frame;
He remembers that we are dust.
As for man, his days are like grass;
As a flower of the field, so he flourishes.

For the wind passes over it, and it is gone,
And its place remembers it no more.
But the mercy of the LORD is from everlasting
  to everlasting
On those who fear Him,
And His righteousness to children's children,
To such as keep His covenant,
And to those who remember His
  commandments to do them.

—PSALM 103:8–18

■ Using Discretion in My Choice of Activities

Do you not know that the unrighteous will not inherit the kingdom of God? Do not be deceived. Neither fornicators, nor idolaters, nor adulterers, nor homosexuals, nor sodomites, nor thieves, nor covetous, nor drunkards, nor revilers, nor extortioners will inherit the kingdom of God. And such were some of you. But you were washed, but you were sanctified, but you were justified in the name of the Lord Jesus and by the Spirit of our God. All things are lawful for me, but all things are not helpful. All things are lawful for me, but I will not be brought under the power of any. Foods for the stomach and the stomach for foods, but God will destroy both it and them. Now the body is not for sexual immorality but for the Lord, and the Lord for the body. And God both raised up the Lord and will also raise us up by His power. Do you not know that your bodies are members of Christ? Shall I then take the members of Christ and make them members of a harlot? Certainly not! Or do you not know that he who is joined to a harlot is one body with her? For "The two," He says, "shall become one flesh." But he who is joined to the Lord is one spirit with Him. Flee sexual immorality. Every sin that a man does is outside the body, but he who commits sexual immorality sins against his own body. Or do you not know that your body is the temple of the Holy Spirit who is in you, whom you have from God, and you are not your own? For you were bought at a price; therefore glorify God in your body and in your spirit, which are God's.

—1 CORINTHIANS 6:9–20

All things are lawful for me, but all things are not helpful; all things are lawful for me, but all things do not edify. Let no one seek his own, but each one the other's well-being.

—1 CORINTHIANS 10:23–24

■ Staying Pure and Free from Uncleanness

Who may ascend into the hill of the LORD?
Or who may stand in His holy place?
He who has clean hands and a pure heart,
Who has not lifted up his soul to an idol,
Nor sworn deceitfully.
He shall receive blessing from the LORD,
And righteousness from the God of his
  salvation.

—PSALM 24:3–5

I will behave wisely in a perfect way.
Oh, when will You come to me?
I will walk within my house with a perfect
    heart.
I will set nothing wicked before my eyes;
I hate the work of those who fall away;
It shall not cling to me.
A perverse heart shall depart from me;
I will not know wickedness.

—PSALM 101:2-4

■ Not Falling Back to Former Ways

But now after you have known God, or rather
are known by God, how is it that you turn again to
the weak and beggarly elements, to which you desire again to be in bondage?

—GALATIANS 4:9

Stand fast therefore in the liberty by which
Christ has made us free, and do not be entangled
again with a yoke of bondage. . . . For you, brethren, have been called to liberty; only do not use
liberty as an opportunity for the flesh, but
through love serve one another.

—GALATIANS 5:1, 13

Therefore we must give the more earnest heed
to the things we have heard, lest we drift away. For
if the word spoken through angels proved steadfast, and every transgression and disobedience received a just reward, how shall we escape if we

neglect so great a salvation, which at the first began to be spoken by the Lord, and was confirmed to us by those who heard Him.

—HEBREWS 2:1–3

Therefore, as the Holy Spirit says:

"Today, if you will hear His voice,
Do not harden your hearts as in the rebellion,
In the day of trial in the wilderness,
Where your fathers tested Me, proved Me,
And saw My works forty years.
Therefore I was angry with that generation,
And said, 'They always go astray in their
   heart,
And they have not known My ways.'
So I swore in My wrath,
'They shall not enter My rest.'"

Beware, brethren, lest there be in any of you an evil heart of unbelief in departing from the living God; but exhort one another daily, while it is called "Today," lest any of you be hardened through the deceitfulness of sin.

—HEBREWS 3:7–13

Therefore do not cast away your confidence, which has great reward.

For you have need of endurance, so that after you have done the will of God, you may receive the promise:

"For yet a little while,
And He who is coming will come and will not
tarry.
Now the just shall live by faith;
But if anyone draws back,
My soul has no pleasure in him."

—HEBREWS 10:35–38

Beloved, I beg you as sojourners and pilgrims, abstain from fleshly lusts which war against the soul.

—1 PETER 2:11

You therefore, beloved, since you know these things beforehand, beware lest you also fall from your own steadfastness, being led away with the error of the wicked; but grow in the grace and knowledge of our Lord and Savior Jesus Christ. To Him be the glory both now and forever. Amen.

—2 PETER 3:17–18

■ Keeping My Brother from Stumbling

Receive one who is weak in the faith, but not to disputes over doubtful things. For one believes he may eat all things, but he who is weak eats only vegetables. Let not him who eats despise him who does not eat, and let not him who does not eat judge him who eats; for God has received him. . . . Therefore let us not judge one another anymore, but rather resolve this, not to put a stumbling block or a cause to fall in our brother's way. I know and am convinced by the Lord Jesus that there is nothing unclean of itself; but to him who considers anything to be unclean, to him it is unclean. Yet if your brother is grieved because of your food, you are no longer walking in love. Do not destroy with your food the one for whom Christ died. Therefore do not let your good be spoken of as evil; for the kingdom of God is not food and drink, but righteousness and peace and joy in the Holy Spirit. . . . It is good neither to eat meat nor drink wine nor do anything by which your brother stumbles or is offended or is made weak. Do you have faith? Have it to yourself before God. Happy is he who does not condemn himself in what he approves.

—ROMANS 14:1–3, 13–17, 21–22

Maintaining Worthy Purposes and Goals

If then you were raised with Christ, seek those things which are above, where Christ is, sitting at the right hand of God. Set your mind on things above, not on things on the earth. For you died, and your life is hidden with Christ in God.

—COLOSSIANS 3:1–3

■ *Living a Life that Has Eternal Significance*

For no other foundation can anyone lay than that which is laid, which is Jesus Christ. Now if anyone builds on this foundation with gold, silver, precious stones, wood, hay, straw, each one's work will become manifest; for the Day will declare it, because it will be revealed by fire; and the fire will test each one's work, of what sort it is. If anyone's work which he has built on it endures, he will receive a reward. If anyone's work is burned, he will suffer loss; but he himself will be saved, yet so as through fire. Do you not know that you are the temple of God and that the Spirit of God dwells in you?

—1 CORINTHIANS 3:11-16

■ *Persevering to the End*

"He who has an ear, let him hear what the Spirit says to the churches. To him who overcomes I will give to eat from the tree of life, which is in the midst of the Paradise of God. . . . He who has an ear, let him hear what the Spirit says to the churches. To him who overcomes I will give some of the hidden manna to eat. And I will give him a white stone, and on the stone a new name written which no one knows except him who receives it. . . . but hold fast what you have till I come. And he who overcomes, and keeps My works until the end, to him I will give power over the nations—

'He shall rule them with a rod of iron;
As the potter's vessels shall be broken to
    pieces'—

as I also have received from My Father; and I
will give him the morning star."

—REVELATION 2:7, 17, 25–28

"He who overcomes shall be clothed in white
garments, and I will not blot out his name from
the Book of Life; but I will confess his name before
My Father and before His angels. . . . Behold, I
come quickly! Hold fast what you have, that no
one may take your crown. He who overcomes, I
will make him a pillar in the temple of My God,
and he shall go out no more. And I will write on
him the name of My God and the name of the city
of My God, the New Jerusalem, which comes
down out of heaven from My God. And I will
write on him My new name. . . . To him who overcomes I will grant to sit with Me on My throne, as I
also overcame and sat down with My Father on
His throne."

—REVELATION 3:5, 11–12, 21

Be strong in the Lord and in the power of His
might. Put on the whole armor of God, that you
may be able to stand against the wiles of the devil.
For we do not wrestle against flesh and blood, but
against principalities, against powers, against the
rulers of the darkness of this age, against spiritual
hosts of wickedness in the heavenly places. Therefore take up the whole armor of God, that you may
be able to withstand in the evil day, and having
done all, to stand. Stand therefore, having girded
your waist with truth, having put on the breast-

plate of righteousness, and having shod your feet with the preparation of the gospel of peace; above all, taking the shield of faith with which you will be able to quench all the fiery darts of the wicked one. And take the helmet of salvation, and the sword of the Spirit, which is the word of God; praying always with all prayer and supplication in the Spirit, being watchful to this end with all perseverance and supplication for all the saints.

—EPHESIANS 6:10b–18

Living the Life of Praise

The previous chapter stressed maintaining your new lifestyle by meeting your nurture needs daily. Part of that maintenance program involves regular meditation on the Scriptures. That's because a focus on self needs to be balanced with a focus on the creator and preserver of self—God.

Surprisingly, losing ourselves in worship and praise "pays off" in significant inner joy. So here's a chapter just for the joy of it! What better place to go than to the psalms for the epitome of the human heart's expression of adoration for the Almighty?

Praise for the Greatness of Creation

O LORD, our Lord,
How excellent is Your name in all the earth,
You who set Your glory above the heavens!
Out of the mouth of babes and infants
You have ordained strength,

Because of Your enemies,
That You may silence the enemy and the
    avenger.
When I consider Your heavens, the work of
    Your fingers,
The moon and the stars, which You have
    ordained,
What is man that You are mindful of him,
And the son of man that You visit him?
For You have made him a little lower than the
    angels,
And You have crowned him with glory and
    honor.
You have made him to have dominion over the
    works of Your hands;
You have put all things under his feet,
All sheep and oxen—
Even the beasts of the field,
The birds of the air,
And the fish of the sea
That pass through the paths of the seas.
O LORD, our Lord,
How excellent is Your name in all the earth!
                                    —PSALM 8:1-9

The earth is the LORD's, and all its fullness,
The world and those who dwell therein.
For He has founded it upon the seas,
And established it upon the waters.
Who may ascend into the hill of the LORD?
Or who may stand in His holy place? . . .
Lift up your heads, O you gates!

And be lifted up, you everlasting doors!
And the King of glory shall come in.
Who is this King of glory?
The LORD strong and mighty,
The LORD mighty in battle.
Lift up your heads, O you gates!
And be lifted up, you everlasting doors!
And the King of glory shall come in.
Who is this King of glory?
The LORD of hosts,
He is the King of glory.

—PSALM 24:1–10

Praise for the LORD's Voice

Give unto the LORD, O you mighty ones,
Give unto the LORD glory and strength.
Give unto the LORD the glory due to His
     name;
Worship the LORD in the beauty of holiness.
The voice of the LORD is over the waters;
The God of glory thunders;
The LORD is over many waters.
The voice of the LORD is powerful;
The voice of the LORD is full of majesty.
The voice of the LORD breaks the cedars,
Yes, the LORD splinters the cedars of Lebanon.
He makes them also skip like a calf,
Lebanon and Sirion like a young wild ox.
The voice of the LORD divides the flames of
     fire.

The voice of the LORD shakes the wilderness;
The LORD shakes the Wilderness of Kadesh.
The voice of the LORD makes the deer give
    birth,
And strips the forests bare;
And in His temple everyone says, "Glory!"
—PSALM 29:1–9

Praise for Deliverance from Trouble and Enemies

I will bless the LORD at all times;
His praise shall continually be in my mouth.
My soul shall make its boast in the LORD;
The humble shall hear of it and be glad.
Oh, magnify the LORD with me,
And let us exalt His name together.
I sought the LORD, and He heard me,
And delivered me from all my fears.
They looked to Him and were radiant,
And their faces were not ashamed.
This poor man cried out, and the LORD heard
    him,
And saved him out of all his troubles.
The angel of the LORD encamps all around
    those who fear Him,
And delivers them.
Oh, taste and see that the LORD is good;
Blessed is the man who trusts in Him!
—PSALM 34:1–8

I will praise You, O LORD, with my whole
   heart;
I will tell of all Your marvelous works.
I will be glad and rejoice in You;
I will sing praise to Your name, O Most High.
When my enemies turn back,
They shall fall and perish at Your presence.
For You have maintained my right and my
   cause;
You sat on the throne judging in
   righteousness.
You have rebuked the nations,
You have destroyed the wicked;
You have blotted out their name forever and
   ever.

—PSALM 9:1–5

Come, behold the works of the LORD,
Who has made desolations in the earth.
He makes wars cease to the end of the earth;
He breaks the bow and cuts the spear in two;
He burns the chariot in the fire.
Be still, and know that I am God;
I will be exalted among the nations,
I will be exalted in the earth!
The LORD of hosts is with us;
The God of Jacob is our refuge.

—PSALM 46:8–11

Oh, clap your hands, all you peoples!
Shout to God with the voice of triumph!
For the LORD Most High is awesome;

He is a great King over all the earth.
He will subdue the peoples under us,
And the nations under our feet.
He will choose our inheritance for us,
The excellence of Jacob whom He loves. Selah
God has gone up with a shout,
The LORD with the sound of a trumpet.
Sing praises to God, sing praises!
Sing praises to our King, sing praises!
For God is the King of all the earth;
Sing praises with understanding.
God reigns over the nations;
God sits on His holy throne.
The princes of the people have gathered
    together,
The people of the God of Abraham.
For the shields of the earth belong to God;
He is greatly exalted.

—PSALM 47:1-9

Praise for God's Rule over Nature

By awesome deeds in righteousness You will
    answer us,
O God of our salvation,
You who are the confidence of all the ends of
    the earth,
And of the far-off seas;
Who established the mountains by His
    strength,
Being clothed with power;

You who still the noise of the seas,
The noise of their waves,
And the tumult of the peoples.
They also who dwell in the farthest parts are
   afraid of Your signs;
You make the outgoings of the morning and
   evening rejoice.
You visit the earth and water it,
You greatly enrich it;
The river of God is full of water;
You provide their grain,
For so You have prepared it.
You water its ridges abundantly,
You settle its furrows;
You make it soft with showers,
You bless its growth.
You crown the year with Your goodness,
And Your paths drip with abundance.
They drop on the pastures of the wilderness,
And the little hills rejoice on every side.
The pastures are clothed with flocks;
The valleys also are covered with grain;
They shout for joy, they also sing.

—PSALM 65:5–13

The LORD reigns, He is clothed with majesty;
The LORD is clothed,
He has girded Himself with strength.
Surely the world is established, so that it
   cannot be moved.
Your throne is established from of old;
You are from everlasting.

The floods have lifted up, O LORD,
The floods have lifted up their voice;
The floods lift up their waves.
The LORD on high is mightier
Than the noise of many waters,
Than the mighty waves of the sea.
Your testimonies are very sure;
Holiness adorns Your house,
O LORD, forever.

—PSALM 93:1-5

May the glory of the LORD endure forever;
May the LORD rejoice in His works.
He looks on the earth, and it trembles;
He touches the hills, and they smoke.
I will sing to the LORD as long as I live;
I will sing praise to my God while I have my
  being.

—PSALM 104:31-33

Praise for God's Reality over Idols

Why should the Gentiles say,
"Where now is their God?"
But our God is in heaven;
He does whatever He pleases.
Their idols are silver and gold,
The work of men's hands.
They have mouths, but they do not speak;
Eyes they have, but they do not see;
They have ears, but they do not hear;

Noses they have, but they do not smell;
They have hands, but they do not handle;
Feet they have, but they do not walk;
Nor do they mutter through their throat.
Those who make them are like them;
So is everyone who trusts in them. . . .
You who fear the LORD, trust in the LORD;
He is their help and their shield. . . .
The heaven, even the heavens, are the LORD's;
But the earth He has given to the children of
    men.
The dead do not praise the LORD,
Nor any who go down into silence.
But we will bless the LORD
From this time forth and forevermore.
Praise the LORD!

—PSALM 115:2–8, 11, 16–18

Praise for God's Knowledge of My Inner Being

O LORD, You have searched me and known
    me.
You know my sitting down and my rising up;
You understand my thought afar off.
You comprehend my path and my lying
    down,
And are acquainted with all my ways. . . .
How precious also are Your thoughts to me, O
    God!
How great is the sum of them!

If I should count them, they would be more in
  number than the sand;
When I awake, I am still with You.

—PSALM 139:1-3, 17-18

Praise the LORD! Praise the LORD, O my soul!
While I live I will praise the LORD;
I will sing praises to my God while I have my
  being.
Do not put your trust in princes,
Nor in a son of man, in whom there is no
  help.
His spirit departs, he returns to his earth;
In that very day his plans perish.
Happy is he who has the God of Jacob for his
  help,
Whose hope is in the LORD his God.

—PSALM 146:1-5

Praise for God's Providential Care

Praise the LORD!
For it is good to sing praises to our God;
For it is pleasant, and praise is beautiful.
The LORD builds up Jerusalem;
He gathers together the outcasts of Israel.
He heals the broken-hearted
And binds up their wounds.
He counts the number of the stars;
He calls them all by name.

Great is our Lord, and mighty in power;
His understanding is infinite.
The LORD lifts up the humble;
He casts the wicked down to the ground.
Sing to the LORD with thanksgiving;
Sing praises on the harp to our God,
Who covers the heavens with clouds,
Who prepares rain for the earth,
Who makes grass to grow on the mountains.
He gives to the beast its food,
And to the young ravens that cry.
He does not delight in the strength of the
   horse;
He takes no pleasure in the legs of a man.
The LORD takes pleasure in those who fear
   Him,
In those who hope in His mercy.

                     —PSALM 147:1–11

[He] made heaven and earth,
The sea, and all that is in them;
Who keeps truth forever,
Who executes justice for the oppressed,
Who gives food to the hungry.
The LORD gives freedom to the prisoners.
The LORD opens the eyes of the blind;
The LORD raises those who are bowed down;
The LORD loves the righteous.
The LORD watches over the strangers;
He relieves the fatherless and widow;
But the way of the wicked He turns upside
   down.

The LORD shall reign forever—
Your God, O Zion, to all generations.
Praise the LORD!

—PSALM 146:6–10

Praise, Morning and Night

O God, You are my God;
Early will I seek You;
My soul thirsts for You;
My flesh longs for You
In a dry and thirsty land
Where there is no water.

—PSALM 63:1

Awake, lute and harp!
I will awaken the dawn.
I will praise You, O LORD, among the peoples,
And I will sing praises to You among the
    nations.
For Your mercy is great above the heavens,
And Your truth reaches to the clouds.
Be exalted, O God, above the heavens,
And Your glory above all the earth;
That Your beloved may be delivered,
Save with Your right hand, and hear me.

—PSALM 108:2–6

From the rising of the sun to its going down
The LORD's name is to be praised.

—PSALM 113:3

Behold, bless the LORD,
All you servants of the LORD,
Who by night stand in the house of the LORD!
Lift up your hands in the sanctuary,
And bless the LORD.

—PSALM 134:1–3

Praise in the Sanctuary

So I have looked for You in the sanctuary,
To see Your power and Your glory.
Because Your lovingkindness is better than
    life,
My lips shall praise You.
Thus I will bless You while I live;
I will lift up my hands in Your name.
My soul shall be satisfied as with marrow and
    fatness,
And my mouth shall praise You with joyful
    lips.

—PSALM 63:2–5

I will go into Your house with burnt offerings;
I will pay You my vows,
Which my lips have uttered
And my mouth has spoken when I was in
    trouble.
I will offer You burnt sacrifices of fat animals,
With the sweet aroma of rams;
I will offer bulls with goats.
Come and hear, all you who fear God,

And I will declare what He has done for my
   soul.
I cried to Him with my mouth,
And He was extolled with my tongue.
If I regard iniquity in my heart,
The LORD will not hear.
But certainly God has heard me;
He has attended to the voice of my prayer.
Blessed be God,
Who has not turned away my prayer,
Nor His mercy from me!

—PSALM 66:13–20

Praise the LORD!
Praise God in His sanctuary;
Praise Him in His mighty firmament!
Praise Him for His mighty acts;
Praise Him according to His excellent
   greatness!

—PSALM 150:1–2

Praise with Singing and Shouting

Oh come, let us sing to the LORD!
Let us shout joyfully to the Rock of our
   salvation.
Let us come before His presence with
   thanksgiving;
Let us shout joyfully to Him with psalms.
For the LORD is the great God,
And the great King above all gods.

In His hand are the deep places of the earth;
The heights of the hills are His also.
The sea is His, for He made it;
And His hands formed the dry land.
Oh come, let us worship and bow down;
Let us kneel before the LORD our Maker.
For He is our God,
And we are the people of His pasture,
And the sheep of His hand.
                              —PSALM 95:1-7

Oh, sing to the LORD a new song!
For He has done marvelous things;
His right hand and His holy arm have gained
   Him the victory.
The LORD has made known His salvation;
His righteousness He has openly shown in the
   sight of the nations.
He has remembered His mercy and His
   faithfulness to the house of Israel;
All the ends of the earth have seen the
   salvation of our God.
Shout joyfully to the LORD, all the earth;
Break forth in song, rejoice, and sing praises.
Sing to the LORD with the harp,
With the harp and the sound of a psalm,
With trumpets and the sound of a horn;
Shout joyfully before the LORD, the King.
                              —PSALM 98:1-6

Make a joyful shout to the LORD, all you
   lands!

Serve the LORD with gladness;
Come before His presence with singing.
Know that the LORD, He is God;
It is He who has made us, and not we
ourselves;
We are His people and the sheep of His
pasture.
Enter into His gates with thanksgiving,
And into His courts with praise.
Be thankful to Him, and bless His name.
For the LORD is good;
His mercy is everlasting,
And His truth endures to all generations.

—PSALM 100:1-5

Praise with Musical Instruments

Rejoice in the LORD, O you righteous!
For praise from the upright is beautiful.
Praise the LORD with the harp;
Make melody to Him with an instrument of
ten strings.
Sing to Him a new song;
Play skillfully with a shout of joy.
For the word of the LORD is right,
And all His work is done in truth.
He loves righteousness and justice;
The earth is full of the goodness of the LORD.

—PSALM 33:1-5

Praise Him with the sound of the trumpet;
Praise Him with the lute and harp!
Praise Him with the timbrel and dance;
Praise Him with stringed instruments and
    flutes!
Praise Him with loud cymbals;
Praise Him with high sounding cymbals!
Let everything that has breath praise the
    LORD.
Praise the LORD!

—PSALM 150:3–6

Praise, Praise, Praise: from Every Created Thing

Praise Him, all His angels;
Praise Him, all His hosts!
Praise Him, sun and moon;
Praise Him, all you stars of light!
Praise Him, you heavens of heavens,
And you waters above the heavens!
Let them praise the name of the LORD,
For He commanded and they were created.
He has also established them forever and ever;
He has made a decree which shall not pass
    away.
Praise the LORD from the earth,
You great sea creatures and all the depths;
Fire and hail, snow and clouds;
Stormy wind, fulfilling His word;
Mountains and all hills;

Fruitful trees and all cedars;
Beasts and all cattle;
Creeping things and flying fowl;
Kings of the earth and all peoples;
Princes and all judges of the earth;
Both young men and maidens;
Old men and children.
Let them praise the name of the LORD,
For His name alone is exalted;
His glory is above the earth and heaven.
And He has exalted the horn of His people,
The praise of all His saints—
Of the children of Israel,
A people near to Him.
Praise the LORD!

—PSALM 148:2–14

Carrying the Recovery Message to Others

Jesus said it to a man He had just healed: Go home and tell about God's goodness to you.

What about you? Have you experienced some healing? How did it happen? Was it all your doing? Or can you give a word of recommendation to your Higher Power?

"You can't keep it unless you give it away." The ultimate paradox! Yet we know it's true. Ultimately, we want happiness. But we know it will only come when we release our white-knuckled grasp on what we think will get it for us (name your addiction here: _____) and turn our attention to making the lives of others a little more happy.

Thanking God for My Own 'Spiritual Awakening'

It is good to give thanks to the LORD,
And to sing praises to Your name, O Most
   High;
To declare Your lovingkindness in the
   morning,
And Your faithfulness every night,
On an instrument of ten strings,
On the lute,
And on the harp,
With harmonious sound.
For You, LORD, have made me glad through
   Your work;
I will triumph in the works of Your hands.
                              —PSALM 92:1–4

Oh, sing to the LORD a new song!
Sing to the LORD, all the earth.
Sing to the LORD, bless His name;
Proclaim the good news of His salvation from
   day to day.
                              —PSALM 96:1–2

Praise the LORD!
Oh, give thanks to the LORD, for He is good!
For His mercy endures forever.
Who can utter the mighty acts of the LORD?
Or can declare all His praise?

Blessed are those who keep justice,
And he who does righteousness at all times!
—PSALM 106:1-3

Oh, give thanks to the LORD, for He is good!
For His mercy endures forever.
Let the redeemed of the LORD say so,
Whom He has redeemed from the hand of the
enemy.
—PSALM 107:1-2

Oh, that men would give thanks to the LORD
for His goodness,
And for His wonderful works to the children
of men!
Let them sacrifice the sacrifices of
thanksgiving,
And declare His works with rejoicing.
—PSALM 107:21-22

Praise the LORD!
I will praise the LORD with my whole heart,
In the assembly of the upright and in the
congregation.
The works of the LORD are great,
Studied by all who have pleasure in them.
His work is honorable and glorious,
And His righteousness endures forever.
He has made His wonderful works to be
remembered;
The LORD is gracious and full of compassion.
He has given food to those who fear Him;

He will ever be mindful of His covenant.
He has declared to His people the power of
   His works,
In giving them the heritage of the nations.
The works of His hands are verity and justice;
All His precepts are sure.
They stand fast forever and ever,
And are done in truth and uprightness.
He has sent redemption to His people;
He has commanded His covenant forever:
Holy and awesome is His name.
The fear of the LORD is the beginning of
   wisdom;
A good understanding have all those who do
   His commandments.
His praise endures forever.

—PSALM 111:1-10

I will extol You, my God, O King;
And I will bless Your name forever and ever.
Every day I will bless You,
And I will praise Your name forever and ever.
Great is the LORD, and greatly to be praised;
And His greatness is unsearchable.
One generation shall praise Your works to
   another,
And shall declare Your mighty acts.
I will meditate on the glorious splendor of
   Your majesty,
And on Your wondrous works.
Men shall speak of the might of Your awesome
   acts,

And I will declare Your greatness.
They shall utter the memory of Your great
     goodness,
And shall sing of Your righteousness.
The LORD is gracious and full of compassion,
Slow to anger and great in mercy.
The LORD is good to all,
And His tender mercies are over all His
     works.
All Your works shall praise You, O LORD,
And Your saints shall bless You.
They shall speak of the glory of Your
     kingdom,
And talk of Your power,
To make known to the sons of men His
     mighty acts, And the glorious majesty of
     His kingdom. . . .
My mouth shall speak the praise of the LORD,
And all flesh shall bless His holy name
Forever and ever.

—PSALM 145:1–12, 21

And I thank Christ Jesus our Lord who has en-
abled me, because He counted me faithful, putting me into the ministry, although I was formerly
a blasphemer, a persecutor, and an insolent man;
but I obtained mercy because I did it ignorantly in
unbelief. And the grace of our Lord was exceedingly abundant, with faith and love which are in
Christ Jesus. This is a faithful saying and worthy
of all acceptance, that Christ Jesus came into the
world to save sinners, of whom I am chief. How-

ever, for this reason I obtained mercy, that in me
first Jesus Christ might show all longsuffering, as
a pattern to those who are going to believe on Him
for everlasting life.

—1 TIMOTHY 1:12–16

Befriending Those Looking for What's Missing

Out of the depths I have cried to You, O
  LORD;
Lord, hear my voice!
Let Your ears be attentive
To the voice of my supplications.
If You, LORD, should mark iniquities,
O Lord, who could stand?
But there is forgiveness with You,
That You may be feared.
I wait for the LORD, my soul waits,
And in His word I do hope.
My soul waits for the Lord
More than those who watch for the morning—
I say, more than those who watch for the
  morning.

—PSALM 130:1–6

I cry out to the LORD with my voice;
With my voice to the LORD I make my
  supplication.
I pour out my complaint before Him;
I declare before Him my trouble.
When my spirit was overwhelmed within me,

Then You knew my path.
In the way in which I walk
They have secretly set a snare for me.
Look on my right hand and see,
For there is no one who acknowledges me;
Refuge has failed me;
No one cares for my soul.

—PSALM 142:1–4

■ God Can Fill Their Emptiness

Come to Me, all you who labor and are heavy laden, and I will give you rest. Take My yoke upon you and learn from Me, for I am gentle and lowly in heart, and you will find rest for your souls. For My yoke is easy and My burden is light.

—MATTHEW 11:28–30

On the last day, that great day of the feast, Jesus stood and cried out, saying, "If anyone thirsts, let him come to Me and drink. He who believes in Me, as the Scripture has said, out of his heart will flow rivers of living water."

—JOHN 7:37–38

Bless the LORD, O my soul,
And forget not all His benefits:
Who forgives all your iniquities,
Who heals all your diseases,
Who redeems your life from destruction,
Who crowns you with lovingkindness and
   tender mercies,

Who satisfies your mouth with good things,
So that your youth is renewed like the
    eagle's.

—PSALM 103:2-5

The poor shall eat and be satisfied;
Those who seek Him will praise the LORD.
Let your heart live forever! . . .
All the prosperous of the earth
Shall eat and worship;
All those who go down to the dust
Shall bow before Him,
Even he who cannot keep himself alive.

—PSALM 22:26, 29

"Come, eat of my bread
And drink of the wine I have mixed."

—PROVERBS 9:5

"Ho! Everyone who thirsts,
Come to the waters;
And you who have no money,
Come, buy and eat.
Yes, come, buy wine and milk
Without money and without price.
Why do you spend money for what is not
    bread,
And your wages for what does not satisfy?
Listen diligently to Me, and eat what is
    good,
And let your soul delight itself in abundance."

—ISAIAH 55:1-2

"You shall eat in plenty and be satisfied,
And praise the name of the LORD your God,
Who has dealt wondrously with you;
And My people shall never be put to shame."

—JOEL 2:26

Now when one of those who sat at the table with
Him heard these things, he said to Him, "Blessed
is he who shall eat bread in the kingdom of God!"

—LUKE 14:15

For this reason I bow my knees to the Father of
our Lord Jesus Christ, from whom the whole family in heaven and earth is named, that He would
grant you, according to the riches of His glory, to
be strengthened with might through His Spirit in
the inner man, that Christ may dwell in your
hearts through faith; that you, being rooted and
grounded in love, may be able to comprehend
with all the saints what is the width and length
and depth and height—to know the love of Christ
which passes knowledge; that you may be filled
with all the fullness of God.

—EPHESIANS 3:14–19

■ *God Can Give Them the Benefits of Belief Too*

But as many as received Him, to them He gave
the right to become children of God, even to those
who believe in His name: who were born, not of

blood, nor of the will of the flesh, nor of the will of man, but of God.

—JOHN 1:12–13

"Most assuredly, I say to you, he who hears My word and believes in Him who sent Me has everlasting life, and shall not come into judgment, but has passed from death into life."

—JOHN 5:24

There is therefore now no condemnation to those who are in Christ Jesus, who do not walk according to the flesh, but according to the Spirit.

—ROMANS 8:1

Blessed be the God and Father of our Lord Jesus Christ, who according to His abundant mercy has begotten us again to a living hope through the resurrection of Jesus Christ from the dead, to an inheritance incorruptible and undefiled and that does not fade away, reserved in heaven for you, who are kept by the power of God through faith for salvation ready to be revealed in the last time.

—1 PETER 1:3–5

But now Christ is risen from the dead, and has become the firstfruits of those who have fallen asleep. For since by man came death, by Man also came the resurrection of the dead. For as in Adam all die, even so in Christ all shall be made alive.

—1 CORINTHIANS 15:20–22

And you, being dead in your trespasses and the uncircumcision of your flesh, He has made alive together with Him, having forgiven you all trespasses, having wiped out the handwriting of requirements that was against us, which was contrary to us. And He has taken it out of the way, having nailed it to the cross.

—COLOSSIANS 2:13–14

Offering the New Life to Others, Through My 'Walk'

"Let your light so shine before men, that they may see your good works and glorify your Father in heaven."

—MATTHEW 5:16

To the weak I became as weak, that I might win the weak. I have become all things to all men, that I might by all means save some. Now this I do for the gospel's sake, that I may be partaker of it with you. Do you not know that those who run in a race all run, but one receives the prize? Run in such a way that you may obtain it.

And everyone who competes for the prize is temperate in all things. Now they do it to obtain a perishable crown, but we for an imperishable crown. Therefore I run thus: not with uncertainty. Thus I fight: not as one who beats the air. But I discipline my body and bring it into subjection, lest, when I have preached to others, I myself should become disqualified.

—1 CORINTHIANS 9:22–27

Now thanks be to God who always leads us in triumph in Christ, and through us diffuses the fragrance of His knowledge in every place. For we are to God the fragrance of Christ among those who are being saved and among those who are perishing. To the one we are the aroma of death leading to death, and to the other the aroma of life to life. And who is sufficient for these things? For we are not, as so many, peddling the word of God; but as of sincerity, but as from God, we speak in the sight of God in Christ.

—2 CORINTHIANS 2:14–17

For this reason we also, since the day we heard it, do not cease to pray for you, and to ask that you may be filled with the knowledge of His will in all wisdom and spiritual understanding; that you may walk worthy of the Lord, fully pleasing Him, being fruitful in every good work and increasing in the knowledge of God; strengthened with all might, according to His glorious power, for all patience and longsuffering with joy; giving thanks to the Father who has qualified us to be partakers of the inheritance of the saints in the light.

—COLOSSIANS 1:9–12

Walk in the Spirit, and you shall not fulfill the lust of the flesh. For the flesh lusts against the

Spirit, and the Spirit against the flesh; and these are contrary to one another, so that you do not do the things that you wish.

—GALATIANS 5:16-17

This I say, therefore, and testify in the Lord, that you should no longer walk as the rest of the Gentiles walk, in the futility of their mind, having their understanding darkened, being alienated from the life of God, because of the ignorance that is in them, because of the hardening of their heart; who, being past feeling, have given themselves over to licentiousness, to work all uncleanness with greediness.

But you have not so learned Christ, if indeed you have heard Him and have been taught by Him, as the truth is in Jesus: that you put off, concerning your former conduct, the old man which grows corrupt according to the deceitful lusts, and be renewed in the spirit of your mind, and put on the new man which was created according to God, in righteousness and true holiness.

—EPHESIANS 4:17-24

For you were once darkness, but now you are light in the Lord. Walk as children of light (for the fruit of the Spirit is in all goodness, righteousness, and truth), proving what is acceptable to the Lord.

—EPHESIANS 5:8-10

And do this, knowing the time, that now it is high time to awake out of sleep; for now our salvation is nearer than when we first believed. The night is far spent, the day is at hand. Therefore let us cast off the works of darkness, and let us put on the armor of light. Let us walk properly, as in the day, not in revelry and drunkenness, not in licentiousness and lewdness, not in strife and envy. But put on the Lord Jesus Christ, and make no provision for the flesh, to fulfill its lusts.

—ROMANS 13:11–14

For we have spent enough of our past lifetime in doing the will of the Gentiles—when we walked in licentiousness, lusts, drunkenness, revelries, drinking parties, and abominable idolatries.

—1 PETER 4:3

Therefore, since we have this ministry, as we have received mercy, we do not lose heart. But we have renounced the hidden things of shame, not walking in craftiness nor handling the word of God deceitfully, but by manifestation of the truth commending ourselves to every man's conscience in the sight of God.

—2 CORINTHIANS 4:1–2

In all things showing yourself to be a pattern of good works; in doctrine showing integrity, reverence, incorruptibility, sound speech that cannot be condemned, that one who is an opponent may be ashamed, having nothing evil to say of you.

—TITUS 2:7–8

But sanctify the Lord God in your hearts, and always be ready to give a defense to everyone who asks you a reason for the hope that is in you, with meekness and fear; having a good conscience, that when they defame you as evildoers, those who revile your good conduct in Christ may be ashamed.

—1 PETER 3:15–16

Offering the New Life to Others, Through My Words

Now all things are of God, who has reconciled us to Himself through Jesus Christ, and has given us the ministry of reconciliation, that is, that God was in Christ reconciling the world to Himself, not imputing their trespasses to them, and has committed to us the word of reconciliation. Therefore we are ambassadors for Christ, as though God were pleading through us: we implore you on Christ's behalf, be reconciled to God.

—2 CORINTHIANS 5:18–20

Then the eleven disciples went away into Galilee, to the mountain which Jesus had appointed for them. And when they saw Him, they worshiped Him; but some doubted.

Then Jesus came and spoke to them, saying, "All authority has been given to Me in heaven and on earth. Go therefore and make disciples of all the nations, baptizing them in the name of the Father and of the Son and of the Holy Spirit, teaching them to observe all things that I have commanded you; and lo, I am with you always, even to the end of the age." Amen.

—MATTHEW 28:16–20

John answered and said, "A man can receive nothing unless it has been given to him from heaven. You yourselves bear me witness, that I said, 'I am not the Christ,' but, 'I have been sent before Him.' He who has the bride is the bridegroom; but the friend of the bridegroom, who stands and hears him, rejoices greatly because of the bridegroom's voice. Therefore this joy of mine is fulfilled. He must increase, but I must decrease. He who comes from above is above all; he who is of the earth is earthly and speaks of the earth. He who comes from heaven is above all. And what He has seen and heard, that He testifies; and no one receives His testimony. He who has received His testimony has certified that God is true. For He whom God has sent speaks the words of God."

—JOHN 3:27–34

"But you shall receive power when the Holy Spirit has come upon you; and you shall be witnesses to Me in Jerusalem, and in all Judea and Samaria, and to the end of the earth."

—ACTS 1:8

To them God willed to make known what are the riches of the glory of this mystery among the Gentiles: which is Christ in you, the hope of glory.

Him we preach, warning every man and teaching every man in all wisdom, that we may present every man perfect in Christ Jesus. To this end I also labor, striving according to His working which works in me mightily.

—COLOSSIANS 1:27–29

■ *Proclaiming with Boldness*

The Example of Peter

Peter, standing up with the eleven, raised his voice and said to them, "Men of Judea and all who dwell in Jerusalem, let this be known to you, and heed my words. For these are not drunk, as you suppose, since it is only the third hour of the day. But this is what was spoken by the prophet Joel:

'And it shall come to pass in the last days,
    says God,
That I will pour out of My Spirit on all flesh;
Your sons and your daughters shall prophesy,
Your young men shall see visions,
Your old men shall dream dreams.
And on My menservants and on My
    maidservants
I will pour out My Spirit in those days;
And they shall prophesy.
I will show wonders in heaven above
And signs in the earth beneath:
Blood and fire and vapor of smoke.
The sun shall be turned into darkness,

And the moon into blood,
Before the coming of the great and notable day
    of the LORD.
And it shall come to pass that whoever calls
    on the name of the LORD shall be saved.'

"Men of Israel, hear these words: Jesus of Naza-
reth, a Man attested by God to you by miracles,
wonders, and signs which God did through Him
in your midst, as you yourselves also know—Him,
being delivered by the determined purpose and
foreknowledge of God, you have taken by lawless
hands, have crucified, and put to death; whom
God raised up, having loosed the pains of death,
because it was not possible that He should be held
by it. For David says concerning Him:

'I foresaw the LORD always before my face,
For He is at my right hand, that I may not be
    shaken.
Therefore my heart rejoiced, and my tongue
    was glad;
Moreover my flesh also will rest in hope.
Because You will not leave my soul in Hades,
Nor will You allow Your Holy One to see
    corruption.
You have made known to me the ways of life;
You will make me full of joy in Your presence.'

"Men and brethren, let me speak freely to you
of the patriarch David, that he is both dead and
buried, and his tomb is with us to this day. There-

fore, being a prophet, and knowing that God had sworn with an oath to him that of the fruit of his body, according to the flesh, He would raise up the Christ to sit on his throne, he, foreseeing this, spoke concerning the resurrection of the Christ, that His soul was not left in Hades, nor did His flesh see corruption. This Jesus God has raised up, of which we are all witnesses."

—ACTS 2:14–32

The Example of Paul

Then Paul stood up, and motioning with his hand said, "Men of Israel, and you who fear God, listen: The God of this people Israel chose our fathers, and exalted the people when they dwelt as strangers in the land of Egypt, and with an uplifted arm He brought them out of it. Now for a time of about forty years He put up with their ways in the wilderness. And when He had destroyed seven nations in the land of Canaan, He distributed their land to them by allotment. After that He gave them judges for about four hundred and fifty years, until Samuel the prophet. And afterward they asked for a king; so God gave them Saul the son of Kish, a man of the tribe of Benjamin, for forty years. And when He had removed him, He raised up for them David as king, to whom also He gave testimony and said,

'I have found David the son of Jesse, a man after My own heart, who will do all My will.'

"From this man's seed, according to the promise, God raised up for Israel a Savior—Jesus—after John had first preached, before His coming, the baptism of repentance to all the people of Israel. And as John was finishing his course, he said, 'Who do you think I am? I am not He. But behold, there comes One after me, the sandals of whose feet I am not worthy to loose.'

"Men and brethren, sons of the family of Abraham, and those among you who fear God, to you the word of this salvation has been sent. For those who dwell in Jerusalem, and their rulers, because they did not know Him, nor even the voices of the Prophets which are read every Sabbath, have fulfilled them in condemning Him. And though they found no cause for death in Him, they asked Pilate that He should be put to death. Now when they had fulfilled all that was written concerning Him, they took Him down from the tree and laid Him in a tomb. But God raised Him from the dead.

"He was seen for many days by those who came up with Him from Galilee to Jerusalem, who are His witnesses to the people. And we declare to you glad tidings."

—ACTS 13:16–32

■ Encouraging with Gentleness

Brethren, if a man is overtaken in any trespass, you who are spiritual restore such a one in a spirit of gentleness, considering yourself lest you also be tempted. Bear one another's burdens, and so fulfill the law of Christ.

—GALATIANS 6:1–2

Now we exhort you, brethren, warn those who are unruly, comfort the fainthearted, uphold the weak, be patient with all.

—1 THESSALONIANS 5:14

Brethren, if anyone among you wanders from the truth, and someone turns him back, let him know that he who turns a sinner from the error of his way will save a soul from death and cover a multitude of sins.

—JAMES 5:19–20

Scripture Index

Old Testament

New Testament